THE VICTORIA HISTORY OF HAMPSHIRE

HERRIARD

RECORDS OF LIFE AND WORK IN A HAMPSHIRE VILLAGE

ALEX CRAVEN

VICTORIA
COUNTY
HISTORY

Hampshire

First published in the United Kingdom in 2025

by The Hobnob Press,
8 Lock Warehouse, Severn Road, Gloucester GL1 2GA
www.hobnobpress.co.uk

on behalf of the Institute of Historical Research, School of Advanced Studies,
University of London

A Victoria County History Publication

British Library Cataloguing in Publication Data
A catalogue record for this book is available from the British Library

ISBN   978-1-918403-00-8

Typeset in Minion Pro 11/14 pt.
Typesetting and origination by John Chandler

Front cover image: HRO, 44M69/P1/76. Plan of Herriard estate, 1818.

Back cover image: Detail of HRO, 44M69/E6/161, describing Sir Thomas (I) Jervoise's losses in the Civil War.

CONTENTS

LIST OF ILLUSTRATIONS

Figures

Map

FOREWORD

H ERRIARD, HOME TO my ancestors for centuries, is a typical parish on the northern edge of the Hampshire downland, still very rural in nature, with its numerous fields, large woods, and a park landscaped by Humphry Repton in the late 18th century. Home to both ancient farmhouses and modern technologies, the parish and the estate at its heart has always looked towards the future and the need to change, adapt and survive, whilst never losing sight of its past.

We are blessed to have a truly remarkable archive amassed by my family and our antecedents, comprising over 250,000 documents stretching back to the 13th century. It is this collection which makes Herriard extraordinary, giving insight into the lives of the men and women who lived here to an extent impossible for many other parishes. In this way I hope that, besides providing the unique and fascinating tale of the parish, this history of Herriard can provide a model for understanding other parishes less fortunate in their historical records.

The idea of a national series of town and parish histories for every county in England was first mooted at Queen Victoria's Diamond Jubilee in 1897, and the Victoria County History (VCH) was dedicated to her. In 2012, Her late Majesty Queen Elizabeth II agreed to the rededication of the project to mark her own Diamond Jubilee.

Hampshire was the first county to publish a history of each of its parishes in red book volumes (1912) but these contained only leading families, the Church of England and local charities. In 2008 Hampshire became the first county to undertake a complete revision of a parish in the modern VCH style which includes the social, economic and religious history of the ordinary people. This volume is the seventh in the new series to be completed in Hampshire. It follows Mapledurwell (2012), Steventon (2016), Basingstoke, a Medieval Town c.1000–c.1600 (2017), Cliddesden, Hatch and Farleigh Wallop (2018), Dummer and Kempshott (2022), and Basingstoke Reinvented 1800–1925: from Agricultural Town to Manufacturing Centre (2025).

This beautifully illustrated book provides a welcome account of the topography, economy, and people of the parish from the earliest evidence of human settlement to the present day. I am sure this volume will appeal not only to all the people of Herriard – past, present, and future - but also to a much wider audience.

John Jervoise

ACKNOWLEDGEMENTS

THIS WORK HAS been a long time in the making. Draft chapters on the landownership and religious history of the parish were originally written by Gordon Kelvie in 2015. I was subsequently employed in 2019 to revise these chapters and to research the remainder of the book, but work on Herriard was much delayed by the Covid pandemic of 2020 and the cautious reopening of archives across the country in 2021.

Although my name features on the cover, like all VCH Hampshire publications this work is very much a collaborative affair. Besides the drafts of Gordon Kelvie, John Hare generously provided a section on medieval agriculture, drawing upon his previously published study of the Wintney priory accounts. Volunteers provided transcriptions of over 170 wills and inventories preserved at Winchester, and detailed notes on 19th-century census records for the parish. Jonathan Dollery produced the map of the parish. Barbara Large undertook fieldwork with Jean Morrin and provided photographs of important buildings. Overseeing the project, Jean Morrin provided the leadership and direction to see the book through to completion, with the invaluable guidance of Adam Chapman and Ruth Slater at the VCH central office at the Institute of Historical Research, University of London.

As ever, we are indebted to a number of organisations and individuals. In particular, this work would not be possible without the continued support of the staff of the Hampshire Record Office, where the vast majority of our source material is kept. Staff of the National Archives at Kew are also always generous in their assistance, as are the librarians of Lambeth Palace Library. We are grateful to the people of Herriard for accommodating us as we explored their parish, especially those who permitted access to private property in the course of our research. In particular, we must thank Mr John Jervoise of Herriard House for his enthusiastic support of the project, his generosity in providing us with a sweeping tour of the parish and giving us the benefit of his extensive knowledge of his home, and for allowing us to reproduce many documents belonging to his family archive. We are also grateful to the British Newspaper Archive, the Church Conservation Trust and their photographer, Andy Marshall, Hampshire Record Office, the Historic Model Railway Society, the National Archives, Kew, and the National Library of Scotland for permission to reproduce illustrations.

We thank Hampshire Archives Trust for a generous grant of £8.000 to enable this work on the Herriard archives to be completed. We have also benefitted from two other donations for this work.

Once again, we are indebted to John Chandler and Louise Ryland-Epton of Hobnob Press for agreeing to publish this book, after the decision of the University of London Press no longer to publish the VCH Shorts series.

Finally, but by no means least, I would like to thank my wife, Claire, for her unstinting support.

Alex Craven

INTRODUCTION

THE VILLAGE OF HERRIARD is located 4 miles (7 km.) south-east of Basingstoke, and 15 miles (24 km.) north-east of Winchester, on the northern edge of the Hampshire downland. Like its neighbours, it is a very rural parish with an overwhelmingly agricultural history, a character which continues into the present day despite the close proximity of the parish to the growing urban centre of Basingstoke. At the heart of the parish lies Herriard House, the home for over four centuries of the Jervoise family. Their family archive, estimated to contain over 250,000 items,[1] turns this ordinary parish into something extraordinary, permitting us to see the life – and particularly the work – of the inhabitants over the centuries in remarkable detail. In this way this otherwise typical parish can serve as a model for less well documented parishes in the Hampshire downland.

Boundaries

THE BOUNDARIES OF Herriard, partially illustrated in the 17th century and in full in a map of 1730, are ancient and have remained the same down to the present day.[2] The parish, which takes the shape of a trapezoid, was said to measure 2,963 a. (1,199 ha.) in 1840,[3] revised slightly in 1861 to 2,978 a. (1,205 ha.).[4] In several places on the east and the west the boundaries trace the outline of ancient furlongs, suggesting that the common fields predated the division of the land into parishes. Much of the modern western boundary is now defined by Oxleaze Lane, and much of the southern boundary is likewise delineated by the course of the road called the Avenue. In the north and north-east of the parish the boundary follows no discernible features, and the line of the boundary was indicated in 1874 by the location of a series of marked beech trees and thorn bushes.[5]

In the late 16th century, the boundary between Herriard and Bradley was planted with a new hedge,[6] but elsewhere along the southern boundary the commons were undivided from neighbouring parishes. The boundary with Bentworth and Lasham

1   HRO, 44M69.
2   HRO, 44M69/P1/105–8.
3   HRO, 21M65/F7/115/1.
4   Census, 1861.
5   OS Map 6", Hants. XXVII (1874 edn).
6   HRO, 44M69/F2/14/8.

† ▇ Chruch

① Herriard House
② St. Mary's Church
③ Manor Farm
④ Grange Farm
⑤ Hurst Farm
⑥ East Farm
⑦ New Inn
⑧ Hyde's Farm
⑨ Bull's Farm
⑩ Lee Farm
⑪ Cold Harbour
⑫ Hale Farm
⑬ Lane End Farm

Modern Buildings

Ⓐ School
Ⓑ Elderfield House
Ⓒ Brickworks
Ⓓ Site of Railway Station

Arable
Pasture
Woodland
Parish Boundary

0   Mile   1

0   Kilometer   1

CLIDDESDEN PARISH
WINSLADE PARISH
Hen Wood
The Avenue
Herriard Park
ELLISFIELD PARISH
Great Bushy Warren Copse
Herriard
Oxlease Lane
Scratchface Lane
Bagmore Lane
Great Matt's Copse
West Common Wood
Middle Common
BRADLEY PARISH
BENTWORTH PARISH

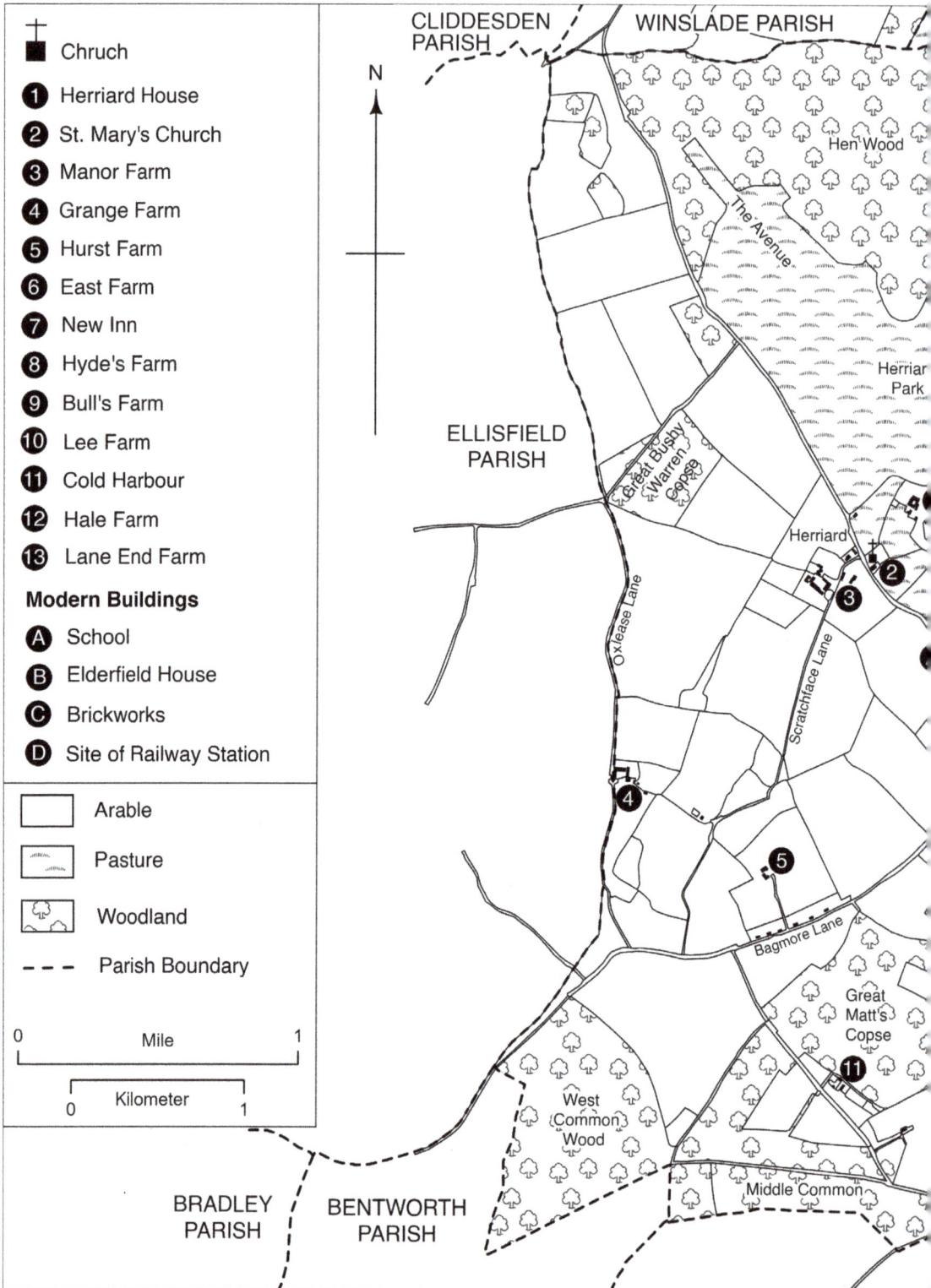

Map 1. Herriard in 1871 (drawn by Jon Dollery).

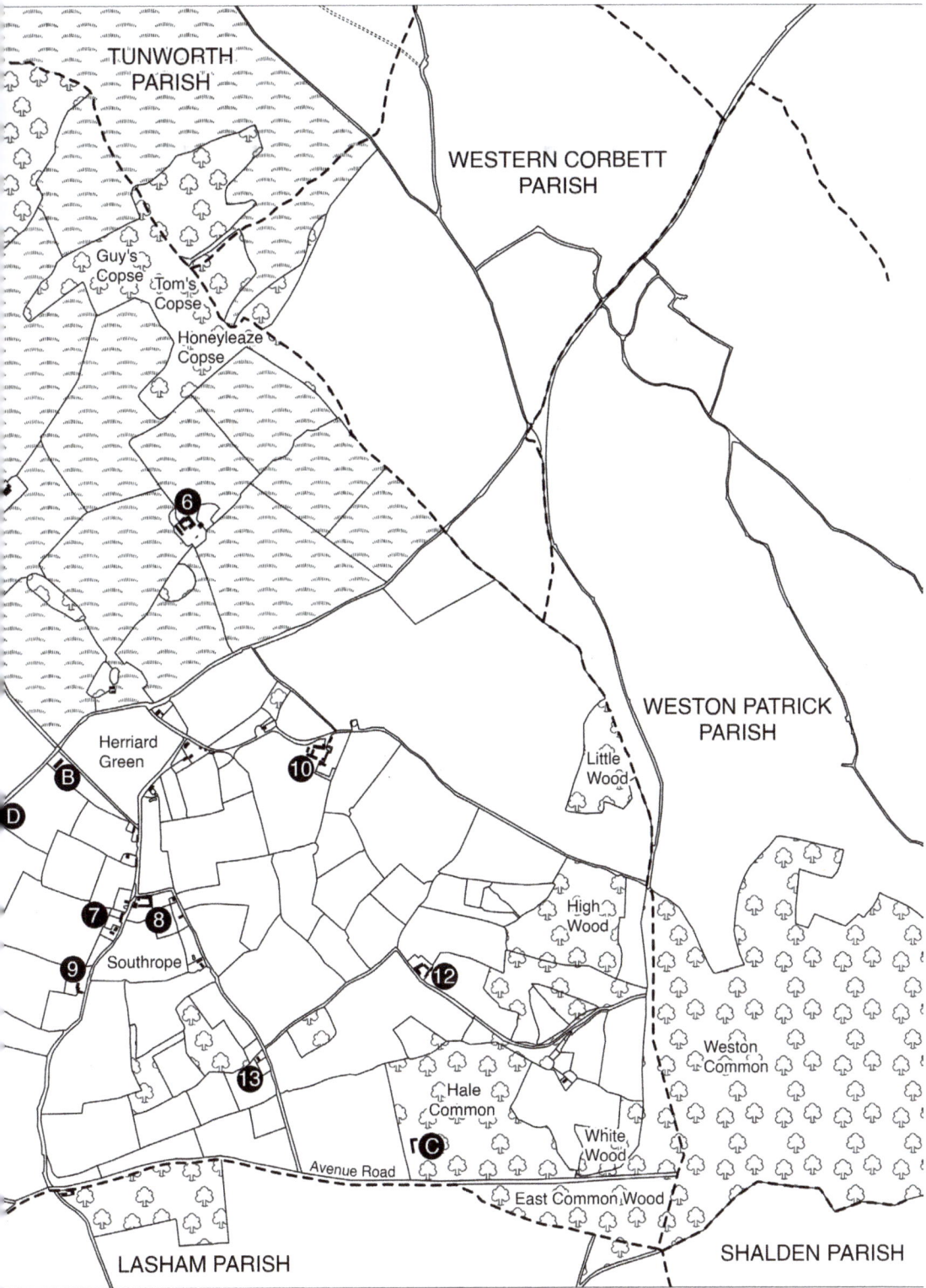

TUNWORTH PARISH

WESTERN CORBETT PARISH

Guy's Copse

Tom's Copse

Honeyleaze Copse

6

Herriard Green

Little Wood

WESTON PATRICK PARISH

B

D

10

7 **8**

9 Southrope

12

High Wood

Weston Common

13

Hale Common

White Wood

C

Avenue Road

East Common Wood

LASHAM PARISH

SHALDEN PARISH

was defined by ditches, green ways, or lines of trees,[7] such as those depicted in a plan of the south-east boundary in 1623.[8] In some places the boundary was marked by crosses in the landscape, such as on the knap of a hill on the boundary with Lasham, and also at a point where Herriard met the boundaries of Shalden and Weston.[9] These various markers took on a ritual significance during the annual perambulation of the boundaries. In the late 16th century readings from the Bible were made at several named trees or other topographical features,[10] and it was presumably one of these trees which gave its name to Gospel Beech field in the early 17th century.[11]

Landscape

THE UNDULATING LANDSCAPE of the parish stands on a plateau of the chalk downland of northern Hampshire, rising to heights of 180m. or more above sea level at Hen Wood, near Herriard House, and south of Southrope, before falling away sharply towards the neighbouring parishes to the north and the east.[12] Over the chalk bedrock, a thick band of clay-with-flints runs from north to south through the centre of the parish, providing the foundation for its principal roads and settlements. Freely draining loamy soils cover most of the parish, giving way to shallow lime-rich soils in on the eastern fringe of the parish, and along Bagmore Lane in the south-west.[13]

The centre of the parish was once occupied by large open fields, but most of these had been enclosed by the early 17th century.[14] Some remnants of these fields were still open in 1730, but were enclosed by agreement in 1738.[15] Interspersed through this landscape are numerous woodlands, including the extensive Hen Wood, first recorded by name in the 13th century and straddling the northern boundary with Tunworth.[16] Large copses lined the eastern boundary in the 16th century, and presumably earlier,[17] and by 1840 almost a quarter of the total area of the parish comprised woodland.[18] Ancient pasture incorporating chalk downland included a large warren, measuring

7   HRO, 44M69/F2/14/8; 44M69/F4/18/27.
8   HRO, 44M69/P1/106.
9   HRO, 44M69/F2/14/8.
10   HRO, 44M69/F2/14/8.
11   HRO, 44M69/F5/4/23.
12   OS Map 1:10000, SU 64 NE (1983 edn).
13   Geol. Surv. Map 1:50,000 (solid and drift), sheet 284 (1981 edn); 'Geology of Britain viewer', http://mapapps.bgs.ac.uk/geologyofbritain/home.html; 'Uk Soil Observatory', http://mapapps2.bgs.ac.uk/ukso/home.html (accessed 12 July 2020).
14   HRO, 44M69/F2/14/8; 44M69/P1/107.
15   HRO, 44M69/P1/108; 44M69/D1/6/M59.
16   HRO, 44M69/C7; 44M69/C287.
17   HRO, 44M69/E2/1/2.
18   HRO, 21M65/F7/115/1–2.

Fig. 1. Herriard House. G.F. Prosser, Select Illustrations of Hampshire (1833).

200 a., north-west of the house.[19] Along the southern boundary of the parish stretched a belt of commons, which had been reduced to bare heathland by the 16th century.[20] By an agreement of *c*.1795 the commons were enclosed and common rights extinguished there,[21] and trees began to be planted on the commons in 1804.[22] The greater part of the commons was still described as furze and bushes in 1840, but they were covered with woodland by 1871,[23] in which state they remain in the present day.

Herriard House has been the focus of several phases of designed landscaes. A lozenge-shaped ditch, enclosing *c*.62 a. surrounding the church and manor, distinguished the medieval manorial complex from the rest of the parish.[24] Several field names within this area refer to a park, and the ditch is still discernible in places. A new house was built in the early 17th century, but was replaced a century later by a grander edifice designed by John James, surrounded by formal gardens designed by George London.[25] Framing the approach to these new grounds from the north was an avenue of silver fir running through Hen Wood to the front of the new house,

19   HRO, 44M69/F2/14/7.
20   HRO, 44M69/F2/14/7; 44M69/F2/14/23; 44M69/P1/106.
21   HRO, 44M69/D1/6/M16–7; 44M69/J9/126.
22   HRO, 44M69/E13/5/32.
23   OS Map 6", Hants. XXVI–XXXVII (1874 edn).
24   HRO, 44M69/P1/107.
25   *ODNB*, 'James, John (*c*.1672–1746), architect, surveyor, and carpenter'; 'London, George (d. 1714), nurseryman and garden designer'; below, Settlement.

probably planted early in the 18th century, and depicted on the map of 1730.[26] The park was greatly expanded after 1794 and landscaped to a design by Humphry Repton, who recommended removing the southern section of the avenue of trees while preserving the northern section 'as a magnificent specimen of the ancient style of gardening'.[27] Arable land north of the house was converted to pasture, while ancient woodland to the north and east of the house was supplemented by the planting of clumps and scattered individual trees.[28] Maps of the early 19th century show the park stretching north from Nashes Green to the edge of Hen Wood, with land to the east of this line still largely under crops.[29] By 1840, however, the park had expanded again to absorb everything to the east of the Basingstoke road and north of the Weston road, including arable land at Bugden, East field, and the northern part of Potshard field. At this time, the park encompassed *c.*880 a. (*c.*356 ha.) within Herriard, of which almost one third (*c.*280 a.) was woodland.[30] The park remained largely pasture and woodland until after the middle of the 20th century, since when large parts have been converted back to arable.

Communications

Roads

Two ancient roads running across the north of the county from Salisbury Plain may have converged at Herriard. The Harroway, a route connecting Cornwall with Kent, has been described as 'the most important of the Hampshire ridgeways'.[31] East of Stonehenge, from which it probably took its name,[32] its route passed through Whitchurch and Oakley before turning south-east to Ellisfield, running across Herriard and continuing towards Farnham (Surr.). The Lunway, the more southerly of the two routes, entered the county to the east of Old Sarum, crossed the Test at Stockbridge, and turned north-east at Totford probably to converge with the Harroway at Herriard.[33] The routes of both roads is uncertain, but it has been conjectured that the Harroway may have run across the parish through Nashes Green and Weston Common towards Golden Pot, perhaps meeting the Lunway at or near Bagmore Lane on its journey from Wield across Herriard Common towards

26   NHLE, no. 1000861, 'Herriard Park'; HRO, 44M69/P1/108. The avenue is also depicted on Isaac Taylor's *Map of Hampshire* (London, 1759).
27   NHLE, no. 1000861, 'Herriard Park'.
28   NHLE, no. 1000861, 'Herriard Park'; HRO, 44M69/E1/1/43.
29   BL, OS Drawings, no. 124, 'Alton' (1808); OS Map 1", Sheet XII (1817 edn).
30   HRO, 21M65/F7/115/1–2.
31   C.F.C. Hawkes, 'Old Roads in Central Hants', *Proc. Hants. F.C.* 9: 3 (1925), 324.
32   Alex Langlands, 'Travel and Communication in the Landscape of Early Medieval Wessex', unpubl. PhD Thesis (University of Winchester, 2013), 118–9.
33   Hawkes, 'Old Roads in Central Hants', 324–6.

Weston.[34] However, alternative routes for both roads might be suggested by the road which formerly ran east from Herriard church towards Weston, obliterated with the extension of Herriard Park but still visible in the landscape, perhaps also incorporating the lane from Bagmore to Herriard church. This latter road, now called Scratchface Lane, was described in a 13th-century deed as the road from Herriard to Winchester.[35] Another deed of the 13th century refers to a road running from Southrope across the heath to Fulflood.[36]

The Basingstoke–Alton road forms the principal route through modern-day Herriard, running north–south through the centre of the parish. The road formed a section of the main route between Oxford and Southampton in the late 17th century, when it ran through Nashes Green and past Lee Farm to Weston common and Golden Pot.[37] The road was turnpiked in 1795 as part of the Basingstoke, Preston Candover and Alton turnpike,[38] when the route was redirected to pass through Southrope and Lasham, necessitating the construction of a new section of road across the fields north of Southrope.[39] The construction of Lasham airfield immediately to the south of the parish boundary during the Second World War caused the diversion of traffic south-west from Middle Common Wood along a circuitous route around the airfield. The road was upgraded in the late 20th century, when a new section was built west of Southrope, bypassing the hamlet.[40]

The Basingstoke road is bisected north of Southrope by a road running between Preston Candover in the west and Weston Patrick in the east. Called Bagmore Lane west of the Basingstoke road and the Street east of it, it was described as the London road in the 18th century.[41] Another road ran east–west across Herriard West Common and Weston common, defining Herrirard's southern boundary with Lasham for much of its length. Described as the road to Odiham in the early 17th century,[42] it was called the Avenue by the early 19th century.[43] A network of smaller lanes connected the parish with its outlying regions and neighbouring communities. Scratchface Lane, from Herriard church to Bagmore, has already been noted. Bushywarren Lane ran west from the Basingstoke road to Ellisfield, whilst a branch of the Lasham road ran south-east from Hydes farm towards the Avenue and East common, becoming the Back lane of Southrope. Besides the former road from Herriard church to Weston Corbett, destroyed by the creation of Herriard Park,

---

34   Hawkes, 'Old Roads in Central Hants', 324–6.
35   HRO, 44M69/C1.
36   HRO, 44M69/C321.
37   Ogliby, *Britannia* (1675), pl. 81; HRO, 44M69/P1/108.
38   Preston Candover to Alton Road Act 1795, 35 Geo. III c. 138.
39   D.J. Viner, 'The Industrial Archaeology of Hampshire Roads: A Survey', *Proc. Hants. F.C.* 26 (1969), 165; HRO, 21M65/F7/115/2.
40   OS Map 1:10000, SU 64 SE (1991 edn).
41   HRO, 44M69/P1/110.
42   HRO, 44M69/P1/105.
43   HRO, 21M65/F7/115/2.

another road once ran across what is now the park towards Tunworth and Winslade, perhaps that mentioned in a deed of 1390.[44]

Basingstoke & Alton Light Railway

Fig. 2. L&SWR H13 railcar no. 1. Reproduced by permission of the Historic Model Railway Society.

Construction of a single-track railway between Basingstoke and Alton began in 1898, the first railway to be authorised under the 1896 Light Railways Act.[45] The line, which ran the length of the parish parallel to the Basingstoke road, opened in 1901 with three services a day in each direction Monday to Saturday,[46] increased to five services a day in 1904.[47] A station with two platforms was constructed in Herriard near the crossing with Bagmore Lane.[48] The railway always operated at a loss and closed in 1917, with the rails subsequently removed and transported to France to assist with the war effort.[49] After the conclusion of the First World War, plans to permanently close the railway met with local opposition,[50] and eventually the track was re-laid and

---

44   HRO, 44M69/C194.
45   TNA, F 4/43; *Hants. & Berks. Gaz.* 19 Dec. 1896; 23 July 1898; Light Railways Act 1896, 59 & 60 Vict. c. 48. Martin Dean, Kevin Robertson, and Roger Simmonds, *The Basingstoke & Alton Light Railway* (Crowcombe, 1998).
46   *Hants. & Berks. Gaz.* 1 June 1901.
47   *Hants. Chron.* 25 June 1904.
48   Dean, Robertson and Simmonds, *Basingstoke & Alton Light Railway*, 95–104.
49   *The Globe*, 21 Dec. 1916; Hansard, House of Commons Debates, 15 July 1918, CVIII, cc. 685–6; *Hants. Telegraph*, 22 Aug. 1924.
50   *Hants. Independent*, 8 Dec. 1922; 29 Dec. 1922; *Hants. Telegraph*, 8 Dec. 1922; 5 Jan. 1923.

the line reopened in 1924, once more with three daily services in each direction.[51] Passenger services were terminated in 1932, with services between Basingstoke and Herriard replaced by buses.[52] Milk and other freight continued to be carried by the railway until its total closure in 1936, when these services were also replaced by road transport.[53]

Carriers, buses and telecommunications

A carter was operating a carrier service in the parish by the early 20th century, and in 1920 he offered scheduled journeys to Basingstoke four days a week.[54]

In the early 20th century bus services in the Basingstoke area were provided by the local operator, Venture. The company was purchased in 1945 by Gloucestershire-based Red & White buses, and transferred in 1950 to the nationalised Wilts. & Dorset Motor Services of Amesbury (Wilts.) when Red & White was sold to the British Transport Commission. In 1952 buses running between Basingstoke and Alton stopped at the New Inn and the parish church in Herriard ten times a day six days a week, with four services on Sundays.[55] Following the creation of the National Bus Company in 1969, all nationalised services in Hampshire were merged under the name of Hants. & Dorset. The Venture name was resurrected for services in the

Fig. 3. Herriard post office in 1908. HRO, 180A12/B1/24.

51 *Hants. Telegraph*, 22 Aug. 1924; 29 Apr. 1932.
52 *Hants. Telegraph*, 9 Sep. 1932.
53 *Hants. Telegraph*, 9 Sep. 1932; 15 May 1936.
54 *Kelly's Dir. Hants.* (1911, 1920 edns).
55 TNA, RAIL 971/168/9.

Basingstoke area early in the late 1970s, until they were placed under the control of a new operating company called Hampshire Bus, acquired by Stagecoach in 1987.

A post office had been established in the village by 1889, and it had become a telegraph and money order office by 1911.[56] Telephone lines were being laid to the village in 1907,[57] and a telephone had been installed at the post office by 1920.[58] Early subscribers included the New Inn, and the Jervoises at Herriard Park, Grange Farm and Manor Farm.[59] A broadband exchange was established at Herriard in 2004,[60] and a fibre network was installed in 2019.[61]

Population

DOMESDAY BOOK RECORDED that there were ten householders (eight villeins and two bordars) and one slave in Herriard. Assuming an average of 4.5 people per household, and depending on whether the local landowner was resident in the parish and whether the slave also had a family, this suggests that the population of Herriard in 1086 was *c*.45–55.[62]

There were 29 taxpayers in the parish *c*.1525, divided almost equally between the two tithings.[63] There were thought to be 109 inhabitants aged 16 or over in Herriard in 1603, suggesting a total population in the parish of under 200.[64] Forty-four households were assessed for the hearth tax *c*.1665, all but six of which were in Southrope, suggesting a decline in settlement in the north of the parish since the early 16th century.[65] There were 81 inhabitants aged 16 or over in 1676, suggesting that the total population had fallen to below 150.[66]

During the 19th century the population of Herriard grew gradually from 330 in 1801 to a peak of 515 in 1851, the highest population in the history of the parish.[67] This growth, an increase of 56 per cent, was driven largely by immigration from the surrounding locality. A total of 288 inhabitants (56 per cent) had been born

56   *Kelly's Dir. Hants.* (1889, 1911 edns).
57   *Hants. Observer & Basingstoke News*, 24 Aug. 1907.
58   *Kelly's Dir. Hants.* (1920 edn).
59   *P.O. Telephone Service Dir.* (1923 edn), II, Section 5, pp. 38–41.
60   *Sam Knows*, https://availability.samknows.com/broadband/exchange/THHD (accessed 12 July 2020).
61   Info. from Mr J. Jervoise, 2025.
62   *Domesday*, 108. For estimating the population from the Domesday survey, see Andrew Hinde, *England's Population* (2003), 15–9.
63   J. Sheail (ed R.W. Hoyle), *The Regional Distribution of Wealth in England as Indicated in the 1524/5 Lay Subsidy Returns*, List & Index Soc. special sers, 29 (1998), pp. 119, 130; TNA, E 179/183/173, rots 12d, 32.
64   *Dioc. Pop. Rtns,* 491.
65   *Hearth Tax, 1665,* 208–9, 218–9.
66   *Compton Census,* 84.
67   Census, 1801; 1851.

in the parish in 1851, whilst another 179 (35 per cent) had been born elsewhere in Hampshire. The remaining 48 residents (9 per cent) were mainly drawn from counties neighbouring Hampshire: Berkshire (six), Surrey (three), Sussex (three), and Wiltshire (nine), including three from Britford, where the Jervoise family also had a house. However, they also included seven from London and Middlesex, five from Ireland, and one from Scotland. The population of the parish was further inflated at this date by the presence of 21 individuals, mostly described as beggars, strollers or vagabonds, living in sheds or outhouses on or near Herriard common.[68]

After the high point of 1851, the population of the parish declined for the following 150 years, falling to 441 in 1861, 406 in 1881, 367 in 1891, and 351 in 1901. By this latter date, the high level of migration ensured that only 110 residents (31 per cent) were natives of the parish, whilst 94 (27 per cent) were not from Hampshire, including the German butler of Herriard House. Nevertheless, most immigration from outside Hampshire was drawn from neighbouring counties, in particular Wiltshire (26). There was also a group of 16 'travelling Gypsies' present in the parish on census day 1901, living under canvas on Bagmore Lane as they travelled from place to place.[69]

The population of Herriard was almost static before the start of the Second World War, but following the war it fell again, to 300 by 1951. It continued to decline over the rest of the 20th century, to 261 in 1971, 230 in 1981, and 215 in 1991. This decline was reversed in the early 21st century, however; in 2011 the population was 251, and ten years later it had risen further to 265.[70]

Settlement

THE EARLIEST EVIDENCE of human activity in Herriard is provided by a Neolithic ground and polished axe-head found near Hen Wood.[71] Another axe-head, this time dating from the Bronze Age, was also found in the parish, although its exact location was not recorded.[72] Other archaeological evidence of the Bronze Age includes a flint scraper found near Bushywarren Lane,[73] and a ring ditch to the east of Park Farm.[74] A short distance to the south of this, close to the road to Weston, lies a distinctively-shaped banjo enclosure of the Iron Age. That this area on the eastern boundary of the modern parish was the focus of prolonged prehistoric settlement is suggested by the name of Potshard field, first recorded early in the 14th century,[75]

68 Census, 1851.
69 Census, 1901.
70 Census, 2011; 2021.
71 HER, 20264.
72 HER, 20251.
73 HER, 67220.
74 HER, 69814.
75 HRO, 44M69/C68–9; 44M69/C84.

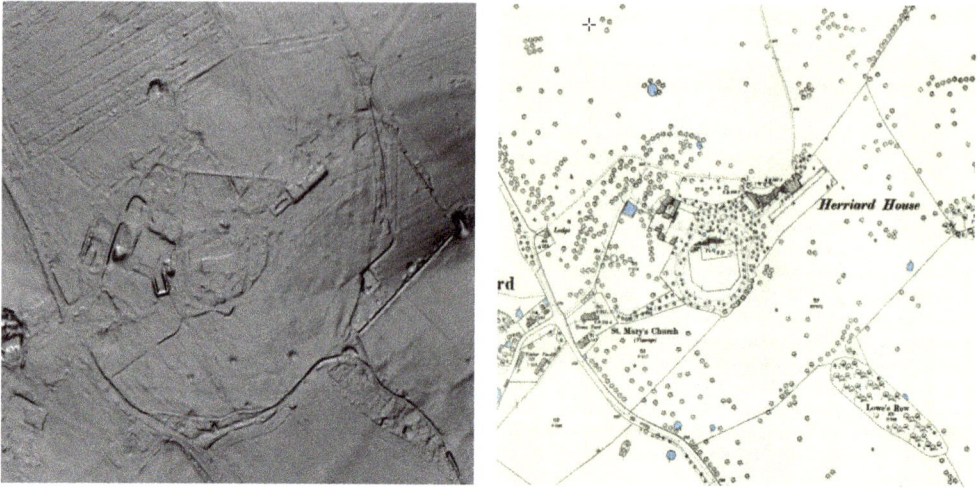

Fig. 4. LIDAR survey and detail from the 1896 Ordnance Survey map (25", Hants. XXVII.5) of the earthworks around Herriard House. Reproduced with the permission of the National Library of Scotland.

referring to the abundant ancient pottery turned up by the ploughs of medieval peasants. On the opposite side of the parish, near Great Bushywarren Copse, the remains of a Roman enclosure hints at early occupation elsewhere in the modern parish.[76]

The name Herriard probably means 'army enclosure' (OE *here* + *geard*), perhaps indicative of a lingering folk memory of the encampment of a 10th-century Danish host,[77] perhaps at or near a possible crossing point of the Harroway and the Lunway.[78] The manor house which once stood near to the present site of the church was presumably an early focus of settlement in the parish. Housing platforms to the north of the church and finds of 13th-century pottery to the south of it suggest the presence of a number of cottages. More pottery and scatters of stone have also been found in the fields around Manor Farm, on the other side of the Basingstoke road from the parish church.[79] The absence of pottery dating from after the 13th century may give an indication of when this area was cleared of dwellings. This coincides with the granting away *c*.1260–70 of two roads, one to Tunworth and the other to Weston, lying near the manor house.[80] The evidence suggests that in the second half of the 13th century everything lying close to the manor was taken in hand by the lord of the manor and enclosed within the lozenge-shaped earthworks surrounding manor house, still visible in the ground, perhaps enclosing the park referred to in the late 13th century.[81] A

76   HER, 33100.
77   Victor Watts, *Cambridge Dictionary of English Place-Names* (Cambridge, 2004).
78   Above, Communications.
79   HER, 20263.
80   HRO, 44M69/C316.
81   HRO, 44M69/C341.

plan of the early 18th century shows these lanes to Weston and Tunworth following a circuitous course around this area, passing to the north of the vacated housing platforms near the church.[82]

The existing evidence suggests that for most of its history settlement has been concentrated in the south of the parish, in particular at Southrope, first referred to in 1168,[83] and described as a hamlet in the 13th century.[84] Now a collection of cottages clustered around the junction of two lanes running south towards Herriard common, housing platforms and earthworks in nearby fields suggest that its full medieval extent was greater than the present day.[85] An area to the east of Southrope known as the Lye, now the site of Lee Farm, was first mentioned in the mid 13th century.[86] Although the modern farm stands isolated, earthworks to its west suggest that this may once have been the focus of a small hamlet.[87] A grange was built near the

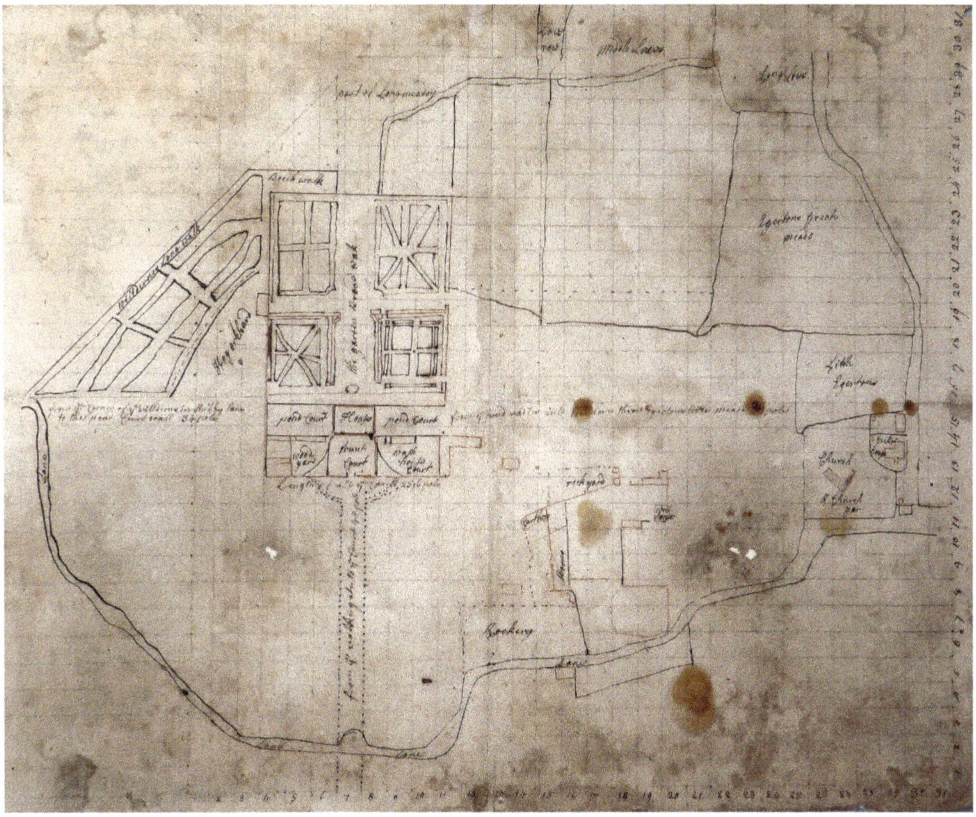

Fig. 5. Sketch by Thomas (II) Jervoise of the grounds around Herriard House, revealing the outline of the medieval enclosure. HRO, 44M69/P1/65.

82   HRO, 44M69/P1/65.
83   *Pipe R.* 14 Hen II (PRS, XII, 1890), 179; *Excerpt. e Rot. Fin.* I, 72; *VCH Hants.* III, 368.
84   HRO, 44M69/C11; 44M69/C221; 44M69/C267.
85   HER, 19175.
86   HRO, 44M69/C5; 44M69/C328; 44M69/C342; 44M69/C349.
87   HER, 20250.

parish boundary with Ellisfield for the priory of Wintney in the middle of the 13th century.[88] Later in the century there were also references to settlement at the Hurst,[89] perhaps the same as that lining the road from Herriard to Bagmore c.1270–80.[90] The names of the Hurst and the Lye both hint at the clearance of woodland to make way for medieval settlement. Also in the late 13th century there are references to a hamlet called Newport.[91] Its location is not known, although it was said to be near the road to Basingstoke, perhaps in an area subsequently absorbed into Herriard Park. Its location may relate to a road called *Portstrete*,[92] said in 1340 to pass through Southrope,[93] and presumably the same road called the Portway in the early 16th century.[94]

Fig. 6. Hydes Farm. © Alex Craven.

If the late Middle Ages was a period of contraction, following the depopulation of the 14th century, the 16th century may represent the beginning of a period of renewal and expansion. In the late 17th century 38 houses in Southrope were assessed for the hearth tax, of which 27 had only one hearth.[95] An estate map of 1730 gives the best indication of the development of the parish in the preceding centuries.[96] It shows the majority of dwellings in the parish lay dispersed along the lanes of Southrope as

88   HRO, 44M69/C1.
89   HRO, 44M69/C1; 44M69/C7; 44M69/C320; 44M69/C349–50.
90   HRO, 44M69/C354.
91   HRO, 44M69/C325.
92   HRO, 44M69/C256; 44M69/C260.
93   HRO, 44M69/C90; 44M69/C95.
94   HRO, 44M69/A1/3/12.
95   *Hearth Tax, 1665*, 208–9.
96   HRO, 44M69/P1/108.

they meandered towards the commons at the southern end of Herriard. The irregular pattern of settlement indicates a lack of planning in their positioning, and particularly at Nashes Green cottages appear to have encroached upon the green. A number of these dwellings, at Golden Dell and along the back lane of Southrope, were first erected in the 17th century,[97] although some may have replaced earlier buildings on the same sites. Amongst the cottages of Southrope stood the more substantial Hydes Farm, at the junction of the ancient road to Lasham and the back lane. The farmhouse itself dates from the late 17th century.[98] Other buildings stood in more isolated positions on the edge of the main settlement or beyond it. Lee Farm, Hurst Farm and Herriard Grange all stood on medieval sites, and Hale's Farm might also have stood on a site of some antiquity. More encroachments were made on the edges of the heaths and woodland clearings that fringed the southern boundary of the parish, where cottages were built from at least the 16th century.[99]

There were fewer buildings in the northern half of the parish. The medieval manor house which had stood near the parish church was said to have been 'utterlie consumed' by a fire in 1597,[100] and a new mansion was erected c.1610–11 on a site to the east of the original house.[101] Some farm buildings apparently remained in use on the site of the former manor house, and the vicarage stood south of the church.[102] There were six houses assessed for the hearth tax in Herriard tithing in 1665, all substantial buildings with between three and six hearths each.[103] Two farmhouses were erected on the demesnes late in the 17th century.[104] The first of these, West or Manor Farm, was built c.1677 to the west of the parish church,[105] whilst the second, East or Park Farm, was built about 20 years later to the east of Herriard House.[106] The mansion house itself was greatly remodelled and extended soon afterwards, work beginning c.1703, probably around the core of the house built a century earlier.[107]

---

97   NHLE, no. 1092959, 'Cotterpins'; no. 1092960, '6, Back Lane'; no. 1092961, 'Lane End'; no. 1092968, 'Golden Dell'; no. 1339520, '2, Back Lane' (accessed 1 Feb. 2021).
98   NHLE, no. 1302154, 'Hydes Farmhouse' (accessed 1 Feb. 2021).
99   HRO, 44M69/D1/6/F2–3; 44M69/F2/14/15; NHLE, no. 1092961, 'Lane End'; no. 1237044, 'Whitewood Cottage'; no. 1322019, 'Chalkdell'; no. 1389452, 'Ash Copse Cottage' (accessed 1 Feb. 2021).
100 HRO, 44M69/G3/55.
101 HRO, 44M69/E4/25–6.
102 HRO, 44M69/P1/65.
103 *Hearth Tax, 1665*, 218–9.
104 HRO, 44M69/P1/107.
105 HRO, 44M69/E7/17; 44M69/D1/6/H1; NHLE, no. 1092973, 'Manor Farmhouse'.
106 HRO, 44M69/D1/6/M48; NHLE, no. 1302191, 'Park Farmhouse'.
107 It has been suggested that Herriard House burnt down in 1703, necessitating its rebuilding, but there appears to be no evidence of a fire, and the 18th-century house incorporated wooden panelling from the earlier house: Prosser, *Select Illustrations of Hampshire* (London, 1833), unpaginated; Sally Jeffery, 'John James and George London at Herriard: Architectural drawings in the Jervoise of Herriard Collection', *Architectural History*, 28 (1985), pp. 40–70.

Fig. 7. Manor Farm. © Alex Craven.

Work on laying out new gardens around the house had already begun in 1699, and would continue for almost a decade.[108] These grounds were significantly remodelled after George Purefoy Jervoise succeeded to the estate in 1792. Following a design by Humphrey Repton, pleasure grounds were laid out to the west of Herriard House, beyond which a large kitchen garden inside high, octagonal walls was constructed, encircled by a walk through exotic trees and shrubs.[109] To the north and south of the house agricultural land was converted into an expanded park landscape, although it did not extend east to envelope Park farm until the 19th century.[110]

New cottages were erected *c.*1827–8 for estate workers at Manor farm and on Bagmore Lane. The were 81 houses in Herriard in 1841, and the number of dwellings in the parish fluctuated very little over the next century.[111] Besides a handful of cottages on new sites, predominantly on the road between Basingstoke and Lasham, a new school was built on the Basingstoke road in 1851, and a new vicarage, called Elderfield House, at the junction of the Basingstoke road and Bagmore Lane by 1871. The construction of the Basingstoke to Alton railway early in the 20th century resulted in the erection of a row of four cottages for railway workers opposite the station. Cottages and a police house were constructed after the Second World War north of the school, bringing the

108 Jeffery, 'James and London at Herriard', 46.
109 NHLE, no. 1000861, 'Herriard Park'.
110 Above, Landscape.
111 Census, 1841.

total number of dwellings in the parish to 88 by 1961.[112]

Developments in the parish since the late 20th century have seen the conversion of former agricultural buildings to commercial or industrial use, and a significant increase of homes in the parish. The alteration of the route of the Basingstoke road to bypass Southrope stimulated the erection of several new houses and bungalows in the attenuated plots created left between the old and new roads. More new houses and a recreation ground with a pavilion were established at Nashes Green, and by 2011 there were 115 dwellings in the parish.[113] In 2025 settlement is scattered in nature, comprising several small pockets of development with no single central focus to the village.

Built Character

OTHER THAN THE 13th-century parish church,[114] there are no extant buildings in the parish known to date from before the 17th century. The character of the village is largely homogenous, irrespective of age and use, with most buildings within

Fig. 8. Church of St Mary, Herriard. © Alex Craven.

112 HRO, 63M83/B24/82; Census, 1961.
113 Census, 2011.
114 Below, Religious History (Church Architecture).

the parish constructed from red brick, especially in Flemish bond, or from flint walls with brick quoins. The majority of older buildings have a timber-framed core, some or all of which is often exposed, whilst some have retained their thatched roofs. Modern development have been limited in scale, consisting of individual properties or a small number of houses. Overall, the size and dispersal of the houses and cottages of Herriard gives the impression of a small, spacious and prosperous village with a significant number of houses dispersed over the parish.

Of the older buildings, perhaps the most noteworthy is Hydes Farm, standing at the junction of Back Lane with the main street in Southrope. This large two-storey, 'L'-plan brick farmhouse applies elements of the late-17th-century Caroline style to a practically arranged and positioned building. Facing away from the road, towards the yard, its brick façade has a centrally positioned doorway and decorative brick band at first-floor level. Above the doorway is a sash window. Both are flanked by several windows of different proportions and positions on the ground and first floor. The house's 'L'-plan tiled hipped roof which projects forward from the walls and has an additional catslide roof section at the rear. The house would have been one of the more substantial in the parish.[115] Several other dwellings dating from the 17th century stand on Back Lane to the east of Hydes Farm, a mixture of one- and two-storey cottages with exposed timber framing and large dormer windows extending from the attics, several with thatched roofs intact.[116] Coopers Corner

Fig. 9. Cooper's Corner Cottage. © Alex Craven.

---

115 NHLE, no. 1302154, 'Hyde's Farmhouse'; *Pevsner North Hants*, 329.
116 NHLE, no. 1339520, '2 Back Lane'; no. 1092958, '3 Back Lane'; no. 1092959, 'Cotterpins';

Cottage, on the main street of Southrope north of Hydes Farm, is another example of this typical vernacular style, with the timber-framing of the upper storey exposed and filled in with brickwork. Its steep roof would also once have been thatched.[117]

The impression of prosperity is reinforced by the construction from the late 17th century onwards of several substantial farmhouses, mostly in the northern half of Herriard. These include the two large demesne farms, Manor (formerly West) and Park (formerly East) Farms. Manor Farm is the grander of the two, perhaps reflecting its location near the main entrance to Herriard Park. Constructed in a U-plan, the two-storey red-brick building has a tall, hipped tiled roof with

Fig. 10. Herriard Grange. © Barbara Large.

overhanging eaves, although the only decoration is a brick band separating the two storeys.[118] Park Farm is the plainer of the two, a solid, symmetrical house with double gables topped by large chimney stacks at either end, again constructed of the ubiquitous red brick and roof tiles.[119] The farmhouses of Lee, Hurst and Grange farms all stand on ancient sites, although the present-day buildings all date from the 18th and early 19th centuries, their exteriors giving no hint of any medieval material that may be incorporated within the structures. Grange Farm is by far the

no. 1092960, '6 Back Lane'; no. 1092961, 'Lane End'.

117 NHLE, no. 1229526, 'Coopers Corner Cottage'.

118 NHLE, no. 1092973, 'Manor Farmhouse'.

119 NHLE, no. 1302191, 'Park Farmhouse'.

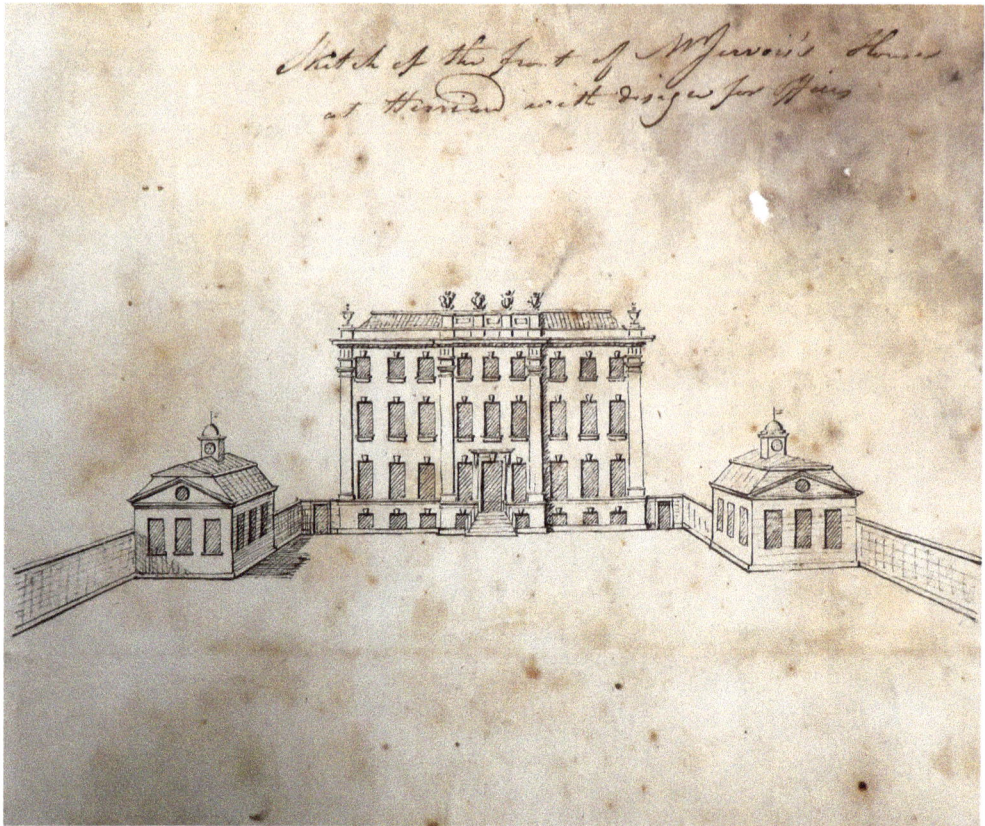

Fig. 11. Sketch of the front of Herriard House, c.1703–4. HRO, 44M69/P1/34.

most impressive, befitting of its status as the farm belonging to the rectory.[120]

There are a number of agricultural buildings also dating from the 18th and 19th centuries, their survival perhaps reflecting more their size and quality of construction rather than an inability to replace them. Most are constructed of a combination of red brick and weatherboarding, for example the 18th-century barn to the east of Hydes Farm.[121] Granaries are raised off the ground on straddles, to protect the contents from vermin. In places these barns have subsequently been adapted for domestic or commercial purposes, but a number of farms continue to work the land.

Little is known about the medieval manor house in Herriard, destroyed by fire c.1596, which stood to the east of the parish church on or near the modern site of Home Farm.[122] The manor house was rebuilt early in the 17th century.[123] It was a substantial building, possessing a gallery, nursery and 14 specified chambers in 1618. In 1614 there was reference to a new building, and in 1618 to a stone court,

120 NHLE, no. 1092971, 'Herriard Grange House'; no. 1178900 'Lee Farmhouse'.
121 NHLE, no. 1302158, 'Barn and Outbuilding to the North-East of Hyde's Farmhouse'.
122 HRO, 44M69/F2/11/20. See HRO, 44M69/E2/16, which locates the manor house near a hop yard. Compare HRO, 44M69/P1/107–8.
123 HRO, 44M69/E4/76; 4M69/E4/77; above, Settlement.

implying that there was more than one courtyard. In 1665 it possessed 25 hearths, making it one of the largest houses in Hampshire.[124] It is depicted in an undated map of the late 17th century on or near its original site, with a large range of stables and farm buildings, and a square structure to the rear, perhaps a walled garden.[125] It was presumably this house which was advertised to let early in the 18th century.[126] By the middle of that century, the house and farm buildings had been replaced by a new range, presumably of agricultural buildings.

By this date a grand mansion had been constructed for Thomas (III) Jervoise in a Baroque style on a new site to the east.[127] Comprising an imposing block of nine bays over two and a half storeys, the house was constructed of brick dressed with stone, with a giant order of Doric pilasters flanking the main entrance and lining the corners of the building. Construction began in 1703 under the direction of the architect John James, his earliest known commission, although Thomas (III) also appears to have taken a close interest in the design of a new house for a decade before this date. Most of the work was completed by 1706, although some work continued until 1711. The building was remodelled twice in the 18th century. There was much internal change in the 1700s, presumably following the inheritance of the estate by Tristram Huddleston Jervoise in 1776. The building was

Fig. 12. Herriard House before demolition, c.1964. HRO, 180A12/B1/24.

124 *Hearth Tax*, 1665, 218.
125 HRO, 44M69/P1/107.
126 HRO, 44M69/M5/7.
127 For the following paras: *Pevsner North Hants*, 52, 329; S. Jeffery, 'John James and George London at Herriard', *Architectural History*, 28 (1985), 40–70; *Country Life*, 1 July 1965.

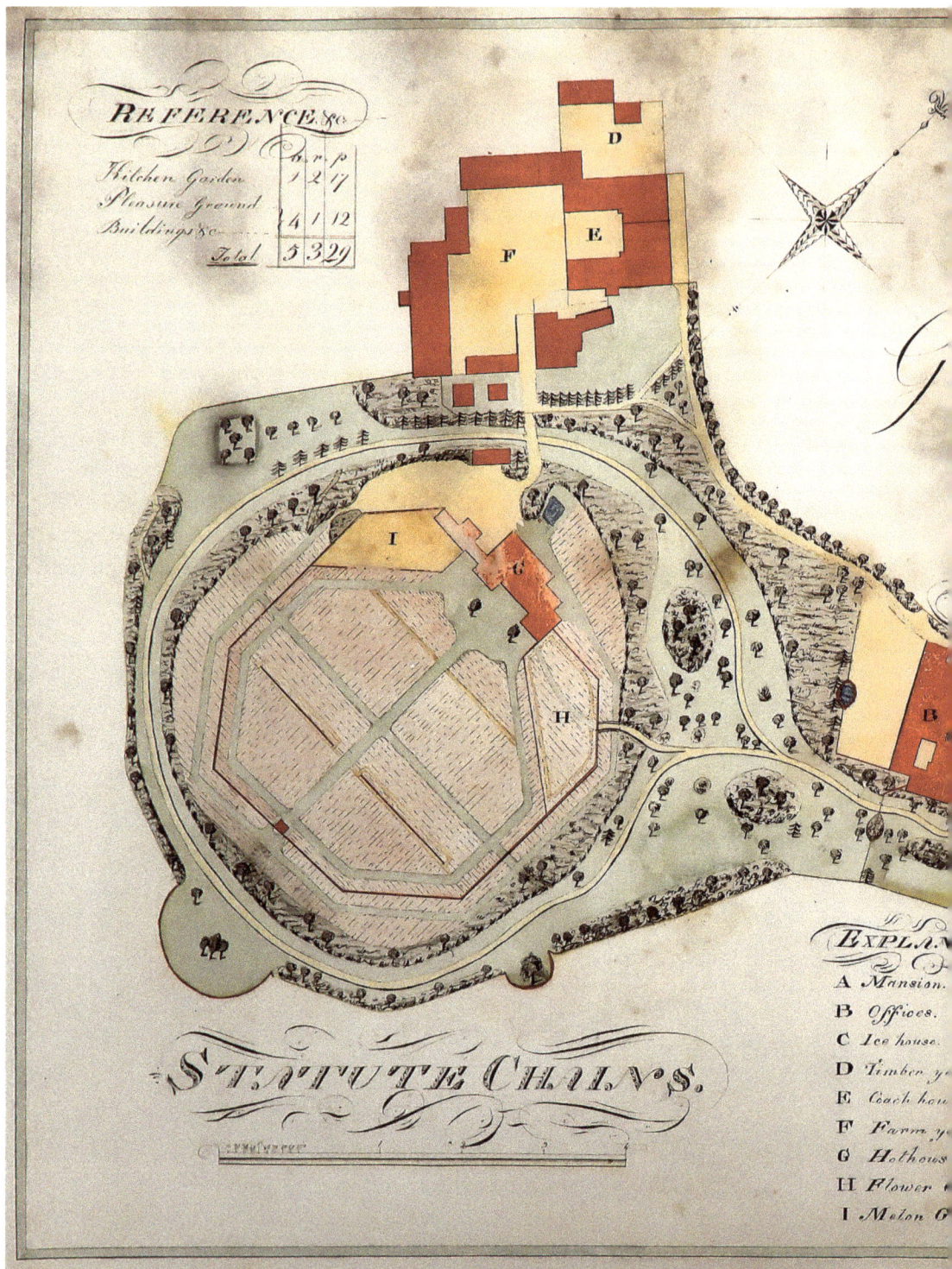

REFERENCE &c

	a	r	p
Kitchen Garden	1	2	17
Pleasure Ground			
Buildings &c	4	1	12
Total	5	3	29

STATUTE CHAINS.

EXPLAN
A Mansion.
B Offices.
C Ice house.
D Timber y
E Coach hou
F Farm y
G Hothous
H Flower
I Melon G

Fig. 13. Plan of Herriard estate, 1818. HRO, 44M69/P1/76.

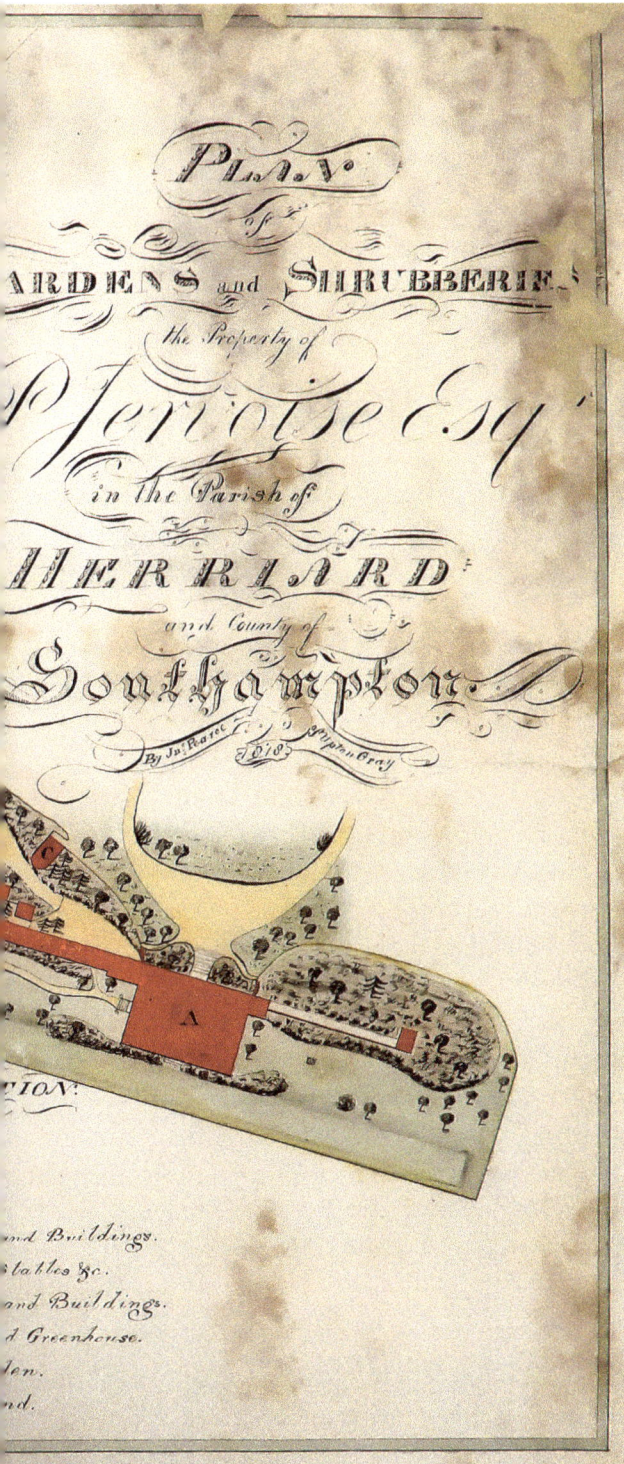

further modified by George Purefoy Jervoise in the 1790s, when a row of office buildings to the east of the houses were demolished, and two symmetrical single-storey wings under tall porticos were added to either side of the house. It was probably then that the brickwork was covered with Roman cement. After the estate passed to John Loveys Jervoise in 1961 the house was deemed too large and expensive to support, and permission was given for its demolition in 1965. A smaller house by Sir Martyn Beckett incorporating some fragments of the older house was erected on the same site in 1966, still occupied by the Jervoise family.

To complement the house extensive formal gardens were laid out around the house, designed by George London between 1699 and 1708. These comprised a series of parterres laid out in symmetrical geometric designs and fountains on a terrace to the rear of the house, and a long avenue of trees leading from the house towards Hackwood House to the north. Both the formal gardens and much of the avenue were swept away in 1796 by George Purefoy Jervoise, who replaced them with a park and pleasure ground, working to designs by Humphrey Repton. At the same time, an octagonal walled kitchen and flower garden was built to the south-west of the house, originally surrounded by a shrubbery walk.

Under the direction of George Purefoy Jervoise improvements were made to the estate, exemplified by the row of seven semi-detached

Fig. 14. One of the model cottages erected by George Purefoy Jervoise on Bagmore Lane.
© Alex Craven.

one- and two-storey symmetrical cottages constructed of red brick in Flemish bond with hipped tiled roofs, erected *c*.1816–21 on Bagmore Lane.[128] More large red brick cottages with tiled roofs were built in the early 19th century on Back Lane in Southrope.[129] The village school was built on the main road in 1851 in a Victorian Gothic style, whilst later in the century the substantial Elderfield House was built at the junction of Bagmore Lane, both using red brick and tiled roofs. Development within the village has remained limited, and new buildings have predominantly used the traditional materials of red brick and tiled roofs. These include a small group of terraced cottages erected for railways workers near Herriard station early in the 20th century, contrasting with the nearby station master's house, with its white rendered walls and numerous gables. Since the 1980s a number of new houses have been built in the parish, although such developments have all been small in scale, such as the eight bungalows erected for pensioners at Nashes Green early in the 1980s,[130] and six semi-detached affordable houses erected on Hockleys Lane *c*.2002.[131] A small number of large private dwellings have been erected in the early 21st century, for example in Bagmore Lane and at Nashes Green.

128   NHLE, nos 1092962–7, '3 Bagmore Lane'; '4, 5 Bagmore Lane'; '6, 7 Bagmore Lane'; '8,9 Bagmore Lane'; '10, 11 Bagmore Lane'; '14, 15 Bagmore Lane'; no. 1178883, '12, 13 Bagmore Lane'.

129 NHLE, no. 1092958, '3 Back Lane'; no. 1093000, 'Southrope Cottage'.

130 BDBC, Planning Portal, Application BDB/14278 (accessed 5 Mar. 2025).

131 Owen White, unpubl. hist. of Herriard, *c*.2002; BDBC, Planning Portal, Application BDB/48583 (accessed 5 Mar. 2025).

LANDOWNERSHIP[132]

HERRIARD WAS HELD before the Norman Conquest by one Erlenc, and by Hugh de Port by the time of the Domesday survey in 1086.[133] Between the 13th and 16th centuries the manor was held by the Coudray family. Thereafter, Herriard descended on two occasions through the female line. In the 16th century the manor came into the hands of Richard Paulet via his wife, Elizabeth Coudray, and in the 17th century Thomas Jervoise became lord of the manor via his wife, Lucy Paulet. As of 2025 the manor of Herriard remains in the hands of the Jervoise family. Various lords of the manor were involved in events of international significance such the Hundred Years Wars, the Dissolution of the Monasteries and the English Civil War while successive lords of Herriard from the 17th to 19th centuries were prominent parliamentarians.

The hamlet of Southrope is also contained within the parish of Herriard, but belonged to the royal manor of Odiham. It was held separately until the mid 13th century, after which it followed the descent of Herriard.

The other major landholder in Herriard until 1536 was Wintney Priory which held the manor of Wintney Herriard Grange. The manor was the product of several grants of land in Herriard, Southrope and Ellisfield to Wintney Priory. After the Dissolution the manor was granted to Sir William Paulet (later 1st marquess of Winchester) and was held by his descendants until it was sold to the Jervoise family in 1851, after which it descended with the manor of Herriard.

During the Middle Ages successive lords of Herriard sub-let parts of their lands in the parish. The survival of leases from the 13th century onwards in the papers of the Jervoise family means that the lesser landholders in Herriard are better documented than would normally be expected.

The Manor of Herriard

Overlordship

Following the Norman Conquest, Herriard formed part of the large Hampshire estate belonging to Hugh de Port, lord of Basing.[134] The honor descended to his son Henry,

---

132 This section was originally written by Gordon McKelvie in 2015, revised by Alex Craven in 2024.
133 *Domesday*, 108.
134 *Domesday*, 108.

sheriff of Hampshire during the reign of Henry I, and then to Henry's younger son John (d. 1167). It was passed to John's son Adam (d. 1213), whose son William took the surname of St John as heir to his maternal grandmother's honor of Halnaker (Suss.).[135] William, who held the lordship in 1235,[136] was succeeded by his son Robert, and grandson John (d. 1302).[137] The latter's son John, who was called to Parliament as baron St John of Basing, died in 1329 holding Herriard amongst his large estates.[138] His son Hugh (d. 1337) was succeeded by his son Edmund, who died in 1347 whilst still a minor.[139] The lordship passed through his sister and coheir, Isabel (d. 1393), to her son Sir Thomas Poynings (d. 1428), whose son Sir Hugh had died in 1426 without a male heir.[140] Following an agreement made in 1458 between Sir Hugh's grandsons, the eldest sons of each of his three daughters, the estates were divided, with the Basing estate passing to John Paulet (d. 1470), the son of Hugh's second daughter Constance and her husband, also John (d. 1429). The estate passed to another John (living 1519), whose son William was created baron St John of Basing in 1539, and marquess of Winchester in 1551.[141] The overlordship of Herriard has not been traced subsequently.

Under the St Johns was an intermediate layer of lordship, held by the FitzPeter family.[142] Herbert, son of Peter, held the manor in 1235, to be succeeded by his brother, Reginald, who held the manor in 1251.[143] Reginald was succeeded in 1286 by his son John, whose son Herbert (d. 1321) held the manor in 1316.[144] His son Matthew held the manor until his death in 1356, when his heirs were his young nieces, daughters of his brother Reginald.[145] The lordship was said in 1524 to be held by Herbert FitzPeter.[146]

The Demesne Manor during the Middle Ages

During the reign of Edward the Confessor the manor was held of the King in alod by his tenant Erlenc. By 1086 the manor was held by Walter,[147] who has been identified

135 I.J. Sanders, *English Baronies: a study of their Origin and descent, 1086–1327* (Oxford, 1960), 9; J.H. Round, 'The Families of St John and of Port', *The Genealogist*, 16 (1899–1900), 1–13. This Adam de Port should not be confused with his contemporary and namesake Adam de Port, lord of Mapledurwell and sheriff of Herefordshire: ibid, 9–10; *Mapledurwell*, 16.
136 TNA, CP 25/1/203/6, no. 176.
137 *Cal. Inq. p.m.* III, 61–62.
138 *Complete Peerage*; *Cal. Inq. p.m.* VII, 185.
139 *Cal. Inq. p.m.* VIII, 52; IX, 37, 39.
140 *Cal. Inq. p.m.* XXIII, 110, 156–60.
141 *Complete Peerage*.
142 *VCH Hants.* III, 367; IV, 270–1.
143 TNA, CP 25/1/203/6, no. 176; HRO, 44M69/C220; *Cal. Inq. p.m.* I, 57–58.
144 *Cal. Inq. p.m.* II, 364–6; V, 274–5; VI, 181; HRO, 44M69/C39.
145 *Cal. Inq. p.m.* VII, 185; VIII, 52; IX, 39; X, 267, 304.
146 TNA, C 142/48/168.
147 *Domesday*, 108.

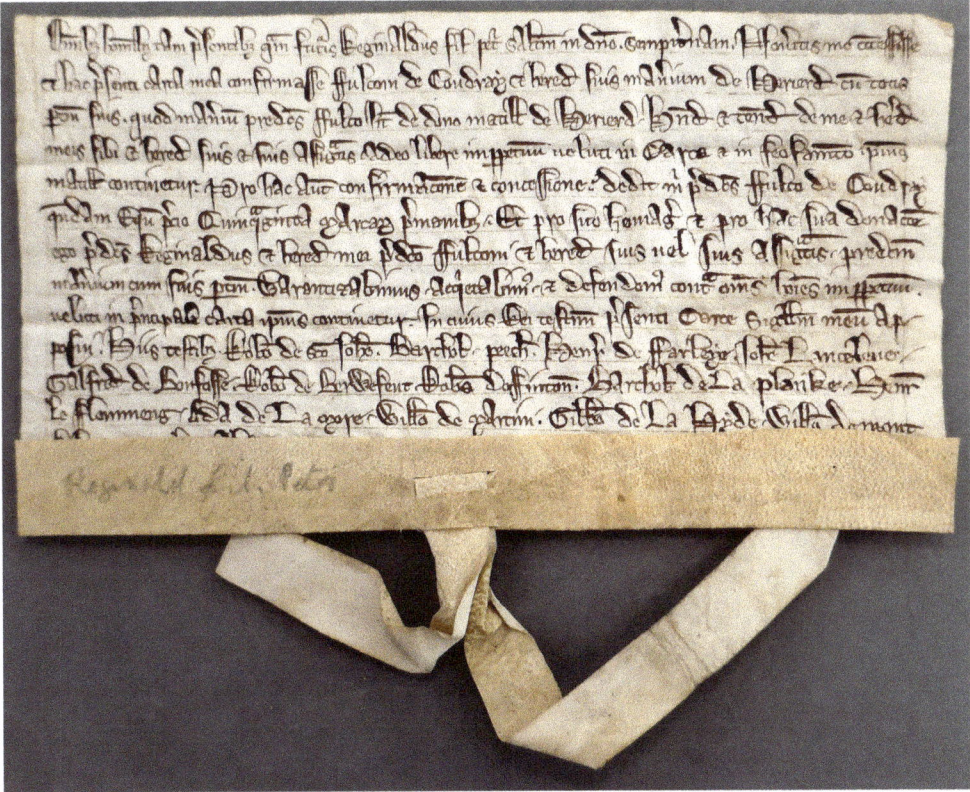

Fig. 15. Grant of the manor of Herriard to Fulc of Coudray, c.1250. HRO, 44M69/C220.

as Walter son of Roger, a major Norman landowner and father of Miles, 1st earl of Hereford.[148] By the 12th century the manor was held by a family who took their name from Herriard. Henry of Herriard was lord in the reign of Henry II,[149] and John of Herriard was lord in the early 13th century. He was succeeded by his son, Richard, whose heir in 1221 was his sister Maud.[150] Her husband Richard of Sifrewast held the manor in 1235 when it was assessed at 1½ knight's fees.[151] Maud and Richard had two sons, Nicholas and Roger, and the latter's son Richard married the mother of Fulk of Coudray. By an agreement of *c.*1250 Maud and her son Nicholas conveyed Herriard to Fulk in exchange for Sherborne Coudray (Hants.) and Padworth (Berks.),[152] for

148 *Prosopography of Anglo-Saxon England*, 'Walter 24', https://domesday.pase.ac.uk/ Domesday?op=5&personkey=42070 (accessed 19 Jan. 2024); K.S.B. Keats-Rohan, *Domesday People: A Prosopography of Persons Occurring in English Documents 1066–1166* (Woodbridge, 1999), 451; *VCH Hants.* I, 425.
149 *Pipe R.* 1167 (PRS 11), 187; *Pipe R.* 1168 (PRS 12), 179.
150 *Cal. Chart.* 1327–41, 393.
151 TNA, CP 25/1/203/6, no. 176.
152 HRO, 44M69/C221–2; 44M69/C228; 44M69/C230. *VCH Berks.* III, 413–4; *VCH Hants.* IV, 160.

confirmation of which Fulk paid 50 marks to Reginald, son of Peter.[153] The manor would remain in the hands of the Coudray family until the 16th century.

When Fulk died in 1251 his heir was his 14-year-old son Peter (later knighted),[154] who conveyed the manor to his son Sir Thomas in 1297.[155] Early in the following year Sir Thomas granted Herriard back to his father for his lifetime,[156] and it remained in Sir Peter's hands until his death c.1303.[157] The manor, assessed in 1316 for a knight's fee,[158] was still held by Sir Thomas in 1346,[159] by which year he had conveyed it to Sir Robert Achard and his wife Agnes for their lifetimes.[160] Sir Thomas died in 1349,[161] and his son Fulk conveyed the reversion of the manor in 1351 to his cousin Henry, to whom Agnes Achard delivered seisin of Herriard in 1354.[162] Henry was still living in 1359, when he was described as lord of the manor,[163] but he had died by 1365, when his widow Joan was granted the manor, presumably as part of her dower.[164]

Henry's heir was his nephew Edward, son of Peter Coudray, who was in possession of the manor in 1366.[165] He may have been the Edward Coudray who was on campaign in 1387 and 1388 with Sir Gilbert Talbot's retinue under the earl of Arundel.[166] Coudray built a career as an administrator, serving as a tax collector for the county in 1388, and then in 1391 entering the service of Bishop Wykeham of Winchester as bailiff of Highclere. He appears to have been close to Wykeham, who left £5 to Coudray in his will, and it was presumably through the bishop's influence that Coudray was elected MP for Hampshire for the first time in 1402, serving in that capacity twice more in 1417 and 1423. He continued to serve on the episcopal estates under Wykeham's successor, Henry Beaufort, although he appears not to have had the same level of intimacy as he had with Wykeham. Away from the bishop's service, Coudray was nominated sheriff of Hampshire twice, in 1404 and

153 HRO, 44M69/C220.
154 *Cal. Inq. p.m.* I, 57–8.
155 HRO, 44M69/C312.
156 TNA, CP 25/1/205/15, no. 225.
157 *Cal. Close*, 1272–1307, 480; HRO, 44M69/C247.
158 HRO, 44M69/C39.
159 The Sir Thomas of Coudray who granted property to his brother Ralph in 1307 is presumably the same Sir Thomas who granted property in 1344 to his brother Ralph: HRO, 44M69/C101, 248. Henry, son of Ralph of Coudray, was described in 1351 as the nephew of Sir Thomas of Coudray: HRO, 44M69C106.
160 *Feudal Aids*, II, 330; HO, 44469/C106; TNA, CP 25/1/206/25, no. 19.
161 *Cal. Inq. p.m.* IX, 171.
162 HRO, 44M69/C267.
163 HRO, 44M69/C135.
164 HRO, 44M69/C274.
165 HRO, 44M69/C276; 44M69/C279; TNA, JUST 1/1476, m. 4. Peter was another son of Ralph of Coudray: HRO, 44M69/C264.
166 TNA, E 101/40/33, m. 12; E 101/41/5, m. 1; *The Medieval Soldier*, http://www.medievalsoldier.org (accessed 19 Oct. 2015).

1417, and was a commissioner of array for the county, as well as serving as sheriff of Berkshire and Oxfordshire in 1412.[167] Coudray died in 1428, to be succeeded by his eldest son Peter,[168] who may previously have served under the duke of Gloucester in 1417.[169] Peter was apparently still alive in 1464, when he delivered seisin of lands in Basingstoke to his son Edward.[170] Whether Edward ever held Herriard is unclear, and he was dead by 1465.[171] Edward's heir Peter, still a minor on his father's death,[172] died in 1527 without a male heir, bringing the Coudray's possession of the manor to an end.

Paulet Family

Following Peter Coudray's death his widow Dorothy took possession of the manor but died soon after, leaving as coheirs their three underage daughters Joan, Margaret and Elizabeth.[173] A division of the estate was agreed c.1544 which left Herriard in the possession of Elizabeth and her husband, Richard Paulet.[174] Richard was a senior official in the lucrative Court of Augmentations, no doubt through the influence of his older brother, William Paulet, the future 1st marquess of Winchester.[175] Richard died c.1551, leaving his son John as his heir,[176] although the manor remained the property of Elizabeth during her lifetime. By 1554 she was married a second time, to William Windsor, 2nd lord Windsor, but he died in 1558.[177] Within little more than a year she was married a third time, to George Puttenham.[178] The marriage was an unhappy one, however, and she later accused

167 *Hist. Parl.* 1386–1421, s.v. 'Cowdray, Edward (c.1355–1428) of Herriard, Hants and Padworth, Berks'.

168 *Reg. Chichele*, II, 375–6; HRO, 44M69/C451; *Feudal Aids*, II, 344.

169 TNA, E 101/51/2, m.1; *The Medieval Soldier*, http://www.medievalsoldier.org (accessed 19 Oct. 2015).

170 HRO, 44M69/C463.

171 TNA, C 140/12/15.

172 TNA, C 140/85/60; HRO, 44M69/B5–6; M. Sharp and W.O. Clinton, *A Record of the Parish of Padworth and its Inhabitants* (Reading, 1911), 121–2.

173 HRO, 44M69/C469; TNA, PROB 11/22/510; C 142/48/168.

174 TNA, CP 25/2/37/246/32HENVIIITRIN (130); CP 25/2/37/247/34HENVIIIEASTER (121).

175 *ODNB*, 'Paulet, William, first marquess of Winchester (1474/5?–1572)' (accessed 19 Oct. 2015); HRO, 44M69/E4/121.

176 TNA, PROB 11/35/54.

177 *Complete Peerage*; *Hist. Parl.* 1509–58, s.v. 'Windsor, William (by 1499–1558), of Bradenham, Bucks'; HRO, 44M69/D1/6/A6. She continued to use the courtesy title Lady Windsor for the rest of her life.

178 *ODNB*, 'Puttenham, George (1529–1590/91)' (accessed 21 Jan. 2024). The following passage is based in part upon this article. Elizabeth and Puttenham were married by April 1560: HRO, 44M69/D1/6/A8.

Fig. 16. Sir Richard Paulet's effigy in Freefolk parish church. © Andy Marshall/Church Conservation Trust.

him of cruelty and adultery with several of her servants.[179] Elizabeth may have first sued Puttenham for divorce in 1566, but it took more than a decade for her to free herself. In the meantime, Puttenham retained possession of the manor whilst they remained married, exploiting it for as much financial benefit as he could extract from it, to the detriment of Elizabeth and John,[180] whilst repeatedly neglecting to pay sufficient maintenance to Elizabeth. For this offence he was repeatedly jailed, sued in the Court of Arches, and excommunicated, and he was also called before the privy council several times for his actions. In 1574 he illegally conveyed Herriard to his brother-in-law, Sir John Throckmorton, although this was later successfully resisted by John Paulet.[181] Elizabeth was finally successful in her attempts to divorce Puttenham in 1578, a fact remarkable in itself in the 16th century, and a measure of the outrage Puttenham's actions inspired. Nevertheless, Elizabeth's legal disputes with him continued until her death in 1589.[182]

Her son John had died ten years earlier, [183] and the manor thus descended to his

179 HRO, 44M69/F2/14/1.
180 Below, Economic History.
181 HRO, 44M69/C712; 44M69/D1/6/A16; 44M69/F2/14/2.
182 *ODNB*, 'Puttenham, George (1529–1590/91)' (accessed 21 Jan. 2024); HRO, 44M69/F2/14/1
183 TNA, C 142/191/79.

son and Elizabeth's grandson, Richard Paulet (knighted in 1591).[184] Paulet owned other estates in Hampshire, most notably at Freefolk, which was his principal residence until he was able to recover Herriard from Puttenham's tenants, and again after fire destroyed the manor house at Herriard *c*.1598.[185] Richard's efforts to restore his family's fortunes and former estates found him frequently engaged in expensive litigation with neighbours and tenants alike. He was active in local government, serving as sheriff of Hampshire in 1590, justice of the peace from 1593, subsidy commissioner and treasurer for maimed soldiers. He used his own influence at Freefolk and that of his brother-in-law, Sir Henry Wallop, as sheriff, to be elected MP for Whitchurch in 1604, and again in 1614. His diary provides a detailed insight into both the affairs of Parliament and his social life whilst in London, while his extensive notes on Herriard give us the first comprehensive picture of the estate.[186] In 1601 Sir Richard purchased the wardship of the orphan Thomas (I) Jervoise, who was soon after married to Paulet's daughter Lucy.[187] Sir Richard died in 1614 with no male heirs, and the estate descended to Jervoise, whose descendants continue to own it in the 21st century.

Fig. 17. Sir Thomas (I) and Lady Lucy Jervoise. HRO, TOP159/2/2–3.

184 TNA, CP 43/25, rot. 36; TNA, CP 25/2/210/30ELIZIHIL; HRO, 44M69/B18; 44M69/C715; *VCH Hants*. III, 367.
185 HRO, 44M69/D1/5/19; 44M69/E2/16.
186 *Hist. Parl.* 1604–29, s.v. 'Paulet, Sir Richard (*c*.1558–1614), of Freefolk, nr. Whitchurch, Hants'; below, Economic History.
187 HRO, 44M69/F4/18/4–8; 44M69/F4/18/35–42; *Hist Parl.* 1604–29, 'Jervoise, Sir Thomas (1587–1654), of Herriard and Freefolk, Hants'.

Jervoise Family

Jervoise, knighted in 1607, held considerable land in other counties, but made
Herriard his principal seat. Like his father-in-law he was active in public affairs,
serving as a subsidy commissioner and justice of the peace in Hampshire, and as
sheriff in Shropshire in 1612. He maintained the family influence in Whitchurch
to be elected MP in 1621, and he was returned by the borough in every election
until the Long Parliament, when he sat alongside his younger son, Richard. With
his Puritan inclination and his increasing obstruction to the financial exactions
of Charles I, it was perhaps no surprise that he took the Parliamentarian cause.
He served as a commissioner and colonel during the Civil War, and his role in the
early months of the year was apparently prominent enough for him to have been
one of three men excluded from a general pardon offered by the King in November
1642. His sons Thomas and Richard (the MP) both served as captains in the
Parliamentarian army, Richard dying in 1645 whilst Thomas served under Fairfax
in the New Model Army until his discharge in 1646. The elder Jervoise later claimed
to have contributed or lost £15,000 because of his support for Parliament, part of
which he was able to recoup after 1649 from the forfeited estate of the marquess
of Winchester.[188] He died in 1654,[189] when he was succeeded by Capt. Thomas (II)
Jervoise (d. 1693), who was followed by his son, Thomas (III) Jervoise (d. 1743),
both of whom represented the county as Whigs in Parliament.[190]

It was the latter Thomas who was responsible for building a grand new mansion
at Herriard, under the direction of John James and George London, completed
c.1704.[191] His frequent absences from the estate, first during six terms as an
MP between 1691 and 1710, and then between 1711 and 1719 travelling in the
Netherlands, Germany and Switzerland, necessitated the employment of capable
bailiffs to manage his affairs at Herriard.[192] Whilst he was abroad Jervoise's servants
endeavoured to let out Herriard House for a period of years, although it is not clear
if this was ever successful.[193] The behaviour of his eldest son, Thomas (IV) Jervoise
(d. 1776), was an increasing cause for concern, and he was declared a lunatic
c.1719. After the death of the father a committee was established in 1743 charged
with managing Thomas's affairs, headed first by his half-brother, Richard Jervoise

188 G.N. Godwin, *Civil War in Hants.* (1904 edn), 39, 71, 104, 314, 370–1; *Hist. Parl.* 1604–
      29, 'Jervoise, Sir Thomas'; 1640–60, 'Jervoise, Sir Thomas (1587–1654), of Herriard and
      Freefolk, Hants'.
189 TNA, PROB 11/241/599.
190 *Hist. Parl.* 1660–1690, s.v. 'Jervoise, Thomas (1616–93), of Herriard, Hants'; 1690–1715, s.v.
      'Jervoise, Thomas (1667–1743), of Herriard, Hants'.
191 Above, Introduction (Built Character).
192 HRO, 44M69/F6/2/1–23; 44M69/F6/10/9; A Gallon, 'An 18th-century credit crunch: the
      Jervoise family of Herriard', *Southern History*, 39 (2017), 79–104.
193 HRO, 44M69/F6/2/10; 44M69/F6/2/12; 44M69/F6/2/25; 44M69/F6/2/29; 44M69/M5/7.

of Britford (Wilts.) until his death in 1762, and then by Richard's son Tristram Huddleston Jervoise, who inherited Herriard in 1776. With no children of his own, Jervoise instead turned to his nephew George Purefoy, for whom Tristram had clear ambitions, writing to prime minister Pitt in 1792 that George 'is reported to be a gentleman of tolerable capacity and good behaviour' and that Tristram was 'ambitious of his [George] being a senator'. Despite this George was not elected during his uncle's lifetime, and the estates passed to him on Tristram's death in 1794, when George assumed the surname of Jervoise.[194] George did however serve as an MP, for Salisbury between 1813 and 1818, and then for the county between 1820 and 1826, as well as serving as sheriff of Hampshire in 1830.[195]

When he also died childless in 1847 the estates passed to his sister Mary and her husband Revd Francis Ellis (later Jervoise),[196] descending to their son Francis Jervoise Ellis Jervoise after Mary's death in 1849, and then to his son Francis Michael Ellis Jervoise.[197] He died in 1903, to be succeeded by his son Francis Henry Tristram Jervoise, sheriff of Hampshire in 1912 and a major in the First World War.[198] His younger brother Richard Somervall Jervoise succeeded in 1959, and died in 1961. The estate passed to his second cousin John Loveys, who adopted the surname Jervoise. He was succeeded by his son, also John, in 2016.[199]

Wintney Herriard Grange

WINTNEY HERRIARD GRANGE was a manor created from several grants of land in Herriard, Southrope and Ellisfield to Wintney Priory. Geoffrey FitzPeter, overlord of Herriard, founded the Cistercian priory of Wintney at some point between 1154 and 1171.[200] Although it was the FitzPeter family that founded the priory, much of the land which later formed the priory's manor in Herriard was derived from the Herriard family.[201] Richard of Heriard granted a total of 6 virgates

194 *Hist. Parl.* 1820–1832, s.v. 'Purefoy Jervoise, George (1770–1847), of Herriard House, nr Basingstoke, Hants and The Moat, nr Britford, Wilts.'; TNA, PRO 30/8/148. George's father, Revd George Huddleston Jervoise, had taken the surname Purefoy in 1765 when he had inherited estates from a kinsman, but resumed the name of Jervoise in 1795, after he inherited the family estates in Wiltshire from his brother, Tristram.

195 *Hist. Parl.* 1790–1820, s.v. 'Purefoy Jervoise, George (1770–1847), of Herriard House, Hants'; *Hist. Parl.* 1820–32, s.v. 'Purefoy Jervoise, George'.

196 *Hist. Parl.* 1820–32, 'Purefoy Jervoise, George'; TNA, PROB 11/206/40.

197 *VCH Hants.* III, 367; *The Ancestor*, 3 (1902), 9.

198 *Who Was Who*, s.v. 'Jervoise, Francis Henry Tristam'.

199 *The Times*, 18 Jan. 2016 ; info. from Mr J. Jervoise, 2025.

200 Diana K. Coldicott, *Hants. Nunneries* (Chichester, 1989), 36.

201 John Hare, 'The Nuns of Wintney Priory and their Manor of Herriard', *Hants. Studies*, 70 (2015), 191–200; *VCH Hants.* II, 149–51.

in Herriard to the priory in the early 13th century,[202] and his sister Maud granted the rent of four tenants in Southrope, worth 20s.[203] Other benefactions included ½ virgate in Southrope, granted by Richard Makerel and subsequently confirmed by Richard of Herriard, and 6 a. in Southrope given by Agnes, the daughter of Edith Pechy.[204] In 1259–60 Henry III made an unsuccessful attempt to recover a virgate in Southrope from the prioress, claiming it had been alienated without license.[205] The land was confirmed to the priory by Edward I in 1281, together with 5 marks of rent.[206] The estates of the priory in Herriard were further augmented in 1334 with the grant by Sir Thomas of Coudray of the advowson and rectory estate of Herriard.[207] By 1428 the priory's estate in Herriard and Southrope amounted to half a knight's fee.[208]

The priory was dissolved in 1536, when the estate at Herriard was granted to William Paulet (later 1st marquess of Winchester), brother of Richard Paulet, the lord of Herriard manor and one of the commissioners overseeing the dissolution of Hampshire's monasteries.[209] The estate subsequently descended with the manor of Basing, although it was confiscated together with the other lands of John Paulet, 5th marquess of Winchester by Parliament in 1646 for his royalism and Catholicism. Herriard Grange was purchased by Lieutenant-General Charles Fleetwood in 1652, but it was restored to the marquess with the rest of his estates after the Resoration.[210] The Herriard Grange estate subsequently descended once more with the manor of Basing to William Orde-Powlett, 3rd baron Bolton (d. 1895), who sold the Grange in 1851 to Francis Ellis Jervoise.[211] Thereafter, the Grange has descended with the manor of Herriard.

Southrope

A s a hamlet within the extensive royal manor of Odiham, there is no separate entry for Southrope in the Domesday Book, and Southrope never became a distinct manor of its own. In the late 12th century Southrope was held by Richard le Malle by a grant of Henry II, for the service of keeping a falcon for the king.[212] By the early 13th century the estate was held by the lords of Herriard.

---

202 HRO, 44M69/C292; *Cal. Chart.* 1327–41, 397.
203 HRO, 44M69/C225; *Cal. Inq. p.m.* I, 15–16.
204 *Cal. Chart.* 1257–1300, 256–7; Dugdale, *Mon.* V, 722; HRO, 44M69/C226.
205 TNA, KB 26/168, rot. 8.
206 *Cal. Pat.* 1272–81, 463.
207 Below, Religious History (Advowson).
208 *Feudal Aids*, II, 344.
209 *L&P Hen. VIII*, XI, 155.
210 *ODNB*, 'Paulet, John, fifth marquess of Winchester (1598?–1675)'; *Cal. Comm. Com.* III, 2373.
211 HRO, 44M69/D1/6/K1; 44M69/D1/6/M3.
212 *Cal. Inq. p.m.* I, 15–16.

In 1221 Maud (or Matilda) of Herriard and her husband Richard Sifrewast paid a fine to enter the lands in Southrope that had been held by her late brother, Richard of Herriard.[213] Sifrewast still held Southrope of the manor of Odiham in 1236, when it was valued at 100*s.* a year.[214] After his death, Maud let Southrope to Fulk of Coudray, with the exception of 20*s.* rent from the lands of Walter le Ghelden, William Botild, William Coterpende and Robert the Miller.[215] When Fulk died in 1251 he held Southrope of the King for the service of 10*s.* a year.[216] The hamlet subsequently descended with the manor of Herriard.[217]

213 *Cal. Chart.* 1327–41, 393.
214 *Book of Fees*, II, 1367.
215 HRO, 44M69/C221.
216 *Cal. Inq. p.m.* I, 57–8.
217 E.g. HRO, 44M69/D1/6/A5–7; 44M69/D1/6/A26; 44M69/C704.

ECONOMIC HISTORY

T HE METICULOUS ACCOUNTS kept by the Jervoise family and their servants, preserved at Herriard Park for centuries, permit a singularly comprehensive view of life and work in a typical Hampshire parish. Account books from the late 16th century onwards record the daily tasks of servants and labourers, the crops sown and harvested, the stock reared and sold, and the cost of provisioning the household of a substantial landowner. The value of these records is the insight they give us into agriculture on the edge of the north Hampshire chalklands.

Herriard is fortunate in being a well-documented parish, but the documentation does not deal with the same units at all times. Thus it is the new subsidiary manor belonging to Hartley Wintney priory which provides us with our main medieval documentation, while the manor of Herriard and hamlet of Southrope provide us with most later evidence, particularly in the north of the parish, much of which was demesne land and often farmed in hand by the lords.

Agricultural Landscape

T HE PARISH WAS divided into three main agricultural elements. The first of these was the settlement of Herriard itself, focused on the medieval manor house and church, surrounded by open fields which were enclosed early.[218] The second settlement, Southrope, lay to the south of Herriard and had its own open field system that was only gradually eroded by piecemeal enclosure. The third element was the new manor of Herriard Wintney Grange, which evolved in the 13th and 14th centuries from grants of land in Herriard, Southrope, and neighbouring Ellisfield. The dependence of this manor on newly colonised land in the west of the parish rather than the existing arable fields is reflected in the medieval accounts where the most commonly used place names are those which suggest enclosure, such as *Haynhurst* (an enclosure by a grove), *Revescroft* (the reeve's croft), and *Hethelese* (a pasture by the heath).

The arable land of the parish lies predominantly in a band running across the centre of the parish, sandwiched between pasture and woodland to the north, and heath and downland to the south. The numerous extant medieval deeds from Herriard reveal the names of fields from the late 13th and early 14th centuries. In the

218 HRO, 44M69/P1/108

north of the parish, a field called *Buxlye*, lying alongside the Basingstoke road and containing a windmill,[219] perhaps later gave its name to the Bushy warren.[220] Also in the north of the parish, a messuage and a virgate of land took its name from Hen Wood in the middle of the 13th century,[221] perhaps the field which adjoined Frying Down in Winslade in the 14th century.[222] Three crofts had been made within Hen Wood by the end of the 13th century.[223] Fields referred to in Southrope included Bagmore field (*Baggemeresfeld*),[224] Potshard field (*Potschatesfeld*),[225] Herriard Deane (*la Dene*),[226] North field,[227] and West field.[228] Piecemeal enclosure of the common fields had apparently already begun by the early 14th century, with references to crofts having been made within Bagmore and West fields.[229] Numerous enclosures had been made by the 16th century, particularly in the west of the parish, where it was said that the tenants held land only in several (i.e. separately) and none in the common fields.[230] In the east of the parish enclosure proceeded at a much slower pace, and three common fields remained open in the early 18th century. A map of 1730 depicted a number of small strips still extant within Little field, Potshard field and Weston Hatch field.[231] These fields were enclosed by agreement with the tenants in 1738.[232]

A park had been established at Herriard by the 13th century, presumably the lozenge-shaped enclosure surrounding the manor house, which may have provided pasture for the lord of the manor.[233] Deeds of the 14th century refer to a pasture called *le Doune* lying by the Basingstoke road north of the parish church,[234] and another lying near the same road called the *Litelperk*.[235] By 1561 the parish was said to contain the large amount of 1,300 a. of pasture and meadow, compared with 500 a. of arable, 500 a. of wood and 500 a. of heath and furze.[236] The former warren in the north of the parish was said to have been a barren bushy heath treated as open common for sheep,

219 HRO, 44M69/C62; 44M69/C64; 44M69/C248.
220 HRO, 44M69/E2/21.
221 HRO, 44M69/C286–7.
222 HRO, 44M69/F2/14/39.
223 HRO, 44M69/C243–4.
224 HRO, 44M69/C243.
225 HRO, 44M69/C68–9.
226 HRO, 44M69/C302; 44M69/C333; 44M69/C335.
227 HRO, 44M69/C40; 44M69/C68–9; 44M69/C362.
228 HRO, 44M69/C13; 44M69/C15; 44M69/C68–9.
229 HRO, 44M69/C65.
230 HRO, 44M69/F2/14/7.
231 HRO, 44M69/P1/108.
232 HRO, 44M69/D1/6/M54–9.
233 HRO, 44M69/C341.
234 HRO, 44M69/C79; 44M69/C86.
235 HRO, 44M69/C127; 44M69/C268.
236 HRO, 44M69/D1/6/A9.

Fig. 18. Section of map of 1730, showing Southrope and small strips in Little Field. HRO, 44M69/ P1/108.

cattle, horses and rabbits, until it was taken in hand as demesne pasture *c.*1567.[237] The marquess of Winchester attempted to claim common there for his estate at the Grange but was unsuccessful, and the warren remained enclosed.[238] In the late 16th and early 17th centuries a large amount of pasture ground, including parts of the warren, was improved through marling and converted to arable.[239] More pasture grounds and coppices lying along the boundaries of the commons were grubbed up and converted to arable during the late 17th and early 18th century.[240]

The parish appears always to have contained a considerable amount of woodland, referred to in 1086 as '*ad clausura*' (to enclose), perhaps meaning that it was soon to be fenced, although no indication is given as to the quantity belonging to Herriard.[241] Straddling the northern parish boundary with Tunworth stands the large woodland called Hen Wood, which gave rise to the family name of Hynewood, already established by the middle of the 13th century.[242] The wood itself is presumably

237 HRO, 44M69/E8/2/1/3.
238 HRO, 44M69/F2/14/7–8.
239 Below, Early Modern Farming.
240 TNA, C 22/414/27; HRO, 44M69/P1/108.
241 *Domesday*, 108.
242 HRO, 44M69/C223; 44M69/C236; 44M69/C287.

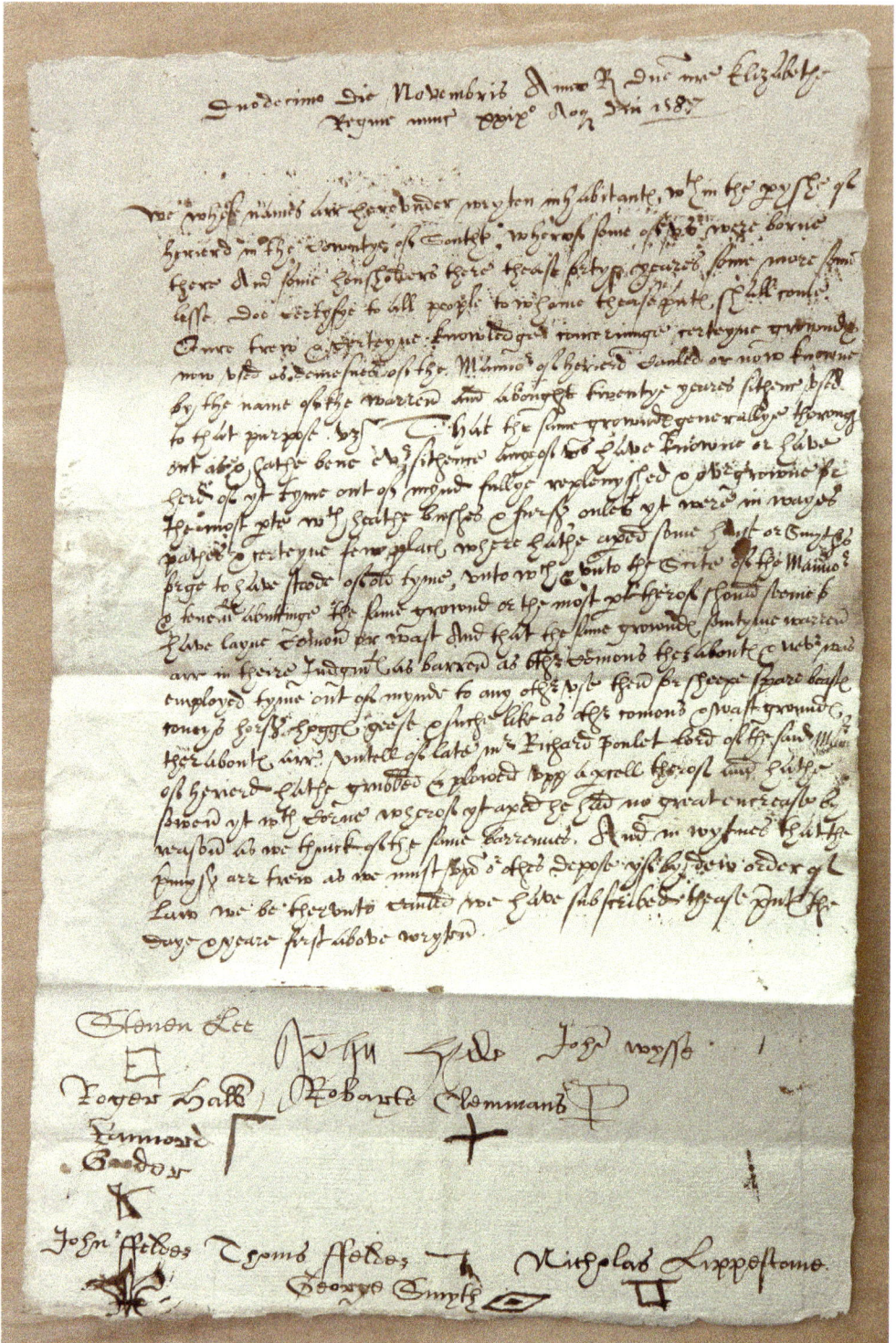

Fig. 19. Petition signed by parishioners about demesne land called the Warren, 1587. HRO, 44M69/E8/2/1/3.

ancient, the name perhaps deriving from the Old English word *heah*, meaning high.[243] More woodland elsewhere in the medieval parish is implied by the place-name Hurst in the south-west of the parish, which occurs by the middle of the 13th century, from the Old English word *hyrst*, meaning wood or wooded hill.[244] Nicholas of the Hurst was granted ½ virgate here in 1259, and Nicholas at Hurst was assessed 18*d*. in the 1327 subsidy.[245] Medieval deeds refer to numerous other small portions of woodland in the hands of tenants.[246] There is also evidence of assarting on the eastern boundary, where a farm called Whitewood was established on the edge of the common by the 16th century.[247] Later maps show a significant amount of woodland in the area, including High Wood and Whitewood coppice, despite having been reduced by numerous small enclosures.[248] Early in the 18th century an avenue of trees was planted parallel to the western boundary of Hen Wood, leading from the Basingstoke road to Herriard House.[249] The planting of Poor Hill, on the north-west edge of Hen Wood, began in the 1720s,[250] although a map of 1730 still shows part of it unplanted and crossed by the Avenue.[251] The rest of Poor Hill was also subsequently planted, and by 1840 the northern section of the Avenue had been obliterated.[252]

Herriard's extensive commons, located on the chalk downlands on the parish's southern boundary and known collectively as Herriard Dingshot (*Herierdingeshet*) in the late 13th century,[253] were said to amount together to about 500 a.[254] By the 16th century they were divided into three, called West heath, Greene Lane heath and Widmore heath. The latter was grazed mostly by tenants who held land in the common fields, whilst the other two, known as the several heaths, were used by tenants who only held enclosed land in the west of the parish.[255] Herriard's commons lay open with those of the neighbouring parishes of Bradley, Lasham and Weston Patrick, and the inhabitants of each had traditionally pastured their sheep and other beasts across the boundaries without any penalty.[256]

The open nature of the commons sparked numerous disputes during the late 16th and early 17th century, in no small part fuelled by the truculent character of Sir Richard Paulet (d. 1614) and his neighbours. During Elizabeth's reign Sir Richard

243 HRO, 10M49/1; G.B. Grundy's notes on Hampshire place-names, II, 85.
244 HRO, 44M69/C1; 44M69/C320; Ekwall, *English Place-Names*, 248.
245 HRO, 44M69/C1; *Hants. Tax List, 1327*, 41.
246 Below, Woodland Management.
247 HRO, 44M69/D1/6/F3; 44M69/P1/108.
248 HRO, 44M69/E7/12; 44M69/P1/108.
249 HRO, 44M69/P1/107–8.
250 HRO, 44M69/E6/167.
251 HRO, 44M69/P1/108.
252 HRO, 21M65/F7/115/2.
253 HRO, 44M69/C219.
254 HRO, 44M69/D1/67/A9; 44M69/F2/14/23.
255 HRO, 44M69/F2/14/7–8.
256 HRO, 44M69/F2/14/8; 44M69/F4/18/23, 27.

Pexall, the lord of Bradley, enclosed his portion of the common with a hedge, apparently with the permission of George Puttenham, who at that time held Herriard in the right of his estranged wife, Lady Elizabeth Windsor (née Coudray).[257] The inhabitants of Herriard subsequently restored access to Bradley common by breaking the hedge, but a new confrontation arose over the common c.1605 when Edward Savage, who then held a portion of Bradley, ordered the hedge to be repaired. The Bradley men were accused at the same time of using dogs to kill some of Sir Richard Paulet's lambs.[258] Paulet complained that Puttenham had had no right to allow the heaths to be divided, having only a life interest in the estate, and also that the new hedge had encroached upon Herriard, wrongly enclosing about 60 a. of West heath into Bradley heath. Savage accused Paulet of inciting his tenants to riot, although the parishioners of Herriard claimed they had merely sought to go on their ancient rogationtide perambulation, reading the gospel and eating cakes in the disputed land.[259]

Further disputes arose c.1622–3 concerning the boundaries with Lasham and Weston,[260] in both cases apparently because Sir Thomas Jervoise had instructed his tenants to plough a furrow marking the boundaries of the commons.[261] Agreement was reached with the marquess of Winchester over the boundary of Weston following arbitration in 1622.[262] The dispute with Sir Edmund Plowdon concerning the boundary with Lasham was more drawn out. In 1623 the men of Lasham were presented in the manorial court of Herriard for encroaching upon c.60 a. of Widmore heath.[263] An agreement was reached whereby two furrows were ploughed to separate the two commons, and the disputed land between them were considered the joint property of both manors.[264] Another dispute concerning an attempt to enclose part of Lasham common c.1665 led to further incidents of hedge-breaking by the men of Herriard.[265] Some parts of the common may have remained open to neighbouring parishes into the 18th century, however, as there were complaints in 1706 that sheep were encroaching on the common from Shalden.[266]

The commons were finally enclosed by agreement with tenants who held rights of pasture there in 1795.[267] Large parts of the commons remained bushes and furze

257 HRO, 44M69/F2/14/23. Writing early in the 17th century, Sir Richard Paulet described it as being '30 or 40 years ago'. Puttenham married Lady Windsor in 1560 and Pexall died in 1571; above, Landownership (Manor of Herriard); *VCH Hants.* IV, 202–5.
258 HRO, 44M69/F2/14/23.
259 HRO, 44M69/F2/14/24; TNA, STAC 8/270/15.
260 HRO, 44M69/F4/18/31.
261 HRO, 44M69/A1/3/13; 44M69/F4/18/25.
262 HRO, 44M69/F4/18/25.
263 HRO, 44M69/A1/3/13.
264 HRO, 44M69/A1/3/15.
265 HRO, 44M69/F5/4/7–8; TNA, C 9/34/74.
266 HRO, 39M89/E/B610/9.
267 HRO, 44M69/D1/6/M16–17; 44M69/J9/126.

in 1840, although *c.*78 a. had been planted with trees and another *c.*14 a. had been broken up for conversion to arable.[268] All three commons had been converted entirely to woodland by 1871.[269]

Agriculture

The Middle Ages

Wintney Priory's manor of Herriard provides us with a well-documented small minor chalkland manor from the period 1335–1426.[270] It was recognised as a grange of the priory from 1329/30. It was close to the priory and served as one of its home manors, providing it with food. Thus in 1397, the priory cellarer received an ox, 12 wethers, 35 ewes, eight pigs, a piglet, eight geese, two goslings, ten capons, 19 hens, 12 chicken and 500 eggs, as well as wheat and oats.[271] At other times it received cheese made from the cow and sheep milk of Herriard, as in 1386/7 and 1416/7.[272]

Four phases of agricultural activity are suggested for the century from 1335. The period from then until the Black Death in 1349 was one of stability, followed by one of shrinkage, instability and experimentation in its aftermath. By contrast the period from 1386 was one of resilience and recovery, leading to peak activity towards the end of the century. After 1405 the instability returned, and our documentation ceased in 1426. The priory then seems to have leased out its manor, but it had probably been resumed by the time of the dissolution of Wintney.[273]

Arable farming at Herriard as elsewhere on the chalkland plateau was dominated by wheat and oats.[274] Here, these two crops usually accounted for at least three-quarters of the sown acreage. The rest was made up of bere, barley and oats, together with a few acres each of beans, peas and vetches. The extent of the sown acreage was about 129 a. in the years 1342–48, although this represented a fall from over 160 a. in 1339 and 1340. The sown acreage fell in the years immediately after the Black Death,

268 HRO, 21M65/F7/115.

269 OS Map 1:2500, Hants. XXVII.9–10 (1873 edn).

270 This section on the Wintney manor or grange was written by J.N. Hare. The evidence is discussed more fully with tabulation of agricultural figures in J.N. Hare, 'The nuns of Wintney Priory and their manor of Herriard: medieval agriculture and settlement in the chalklands of north-east Hampshire', *Proc. Hants. F.C.,* 70 (2015), 191–200. There is also an undated rental, probably dating from earlier in the 14th century: HRO, 44M69/E1/2/48.

271 HRO, 44M69/A1/6/6, m. 4.

272 HRO, 44M69/A1/3/6, mm. 2, 9.

273 TNA, E 178/2018.

274 J. Hare, 'The bishop and the prior: demesne agriculture in medieval Hampshire', *Ag. Hist. Rev.* 54 (2006), 194–6; idem. 'Hampshire agriculture in the Middle Ages: the bishop of Winchester's manor of North Waltham', *Proc. Hants. F.C.* 75 (2020), 67–9.

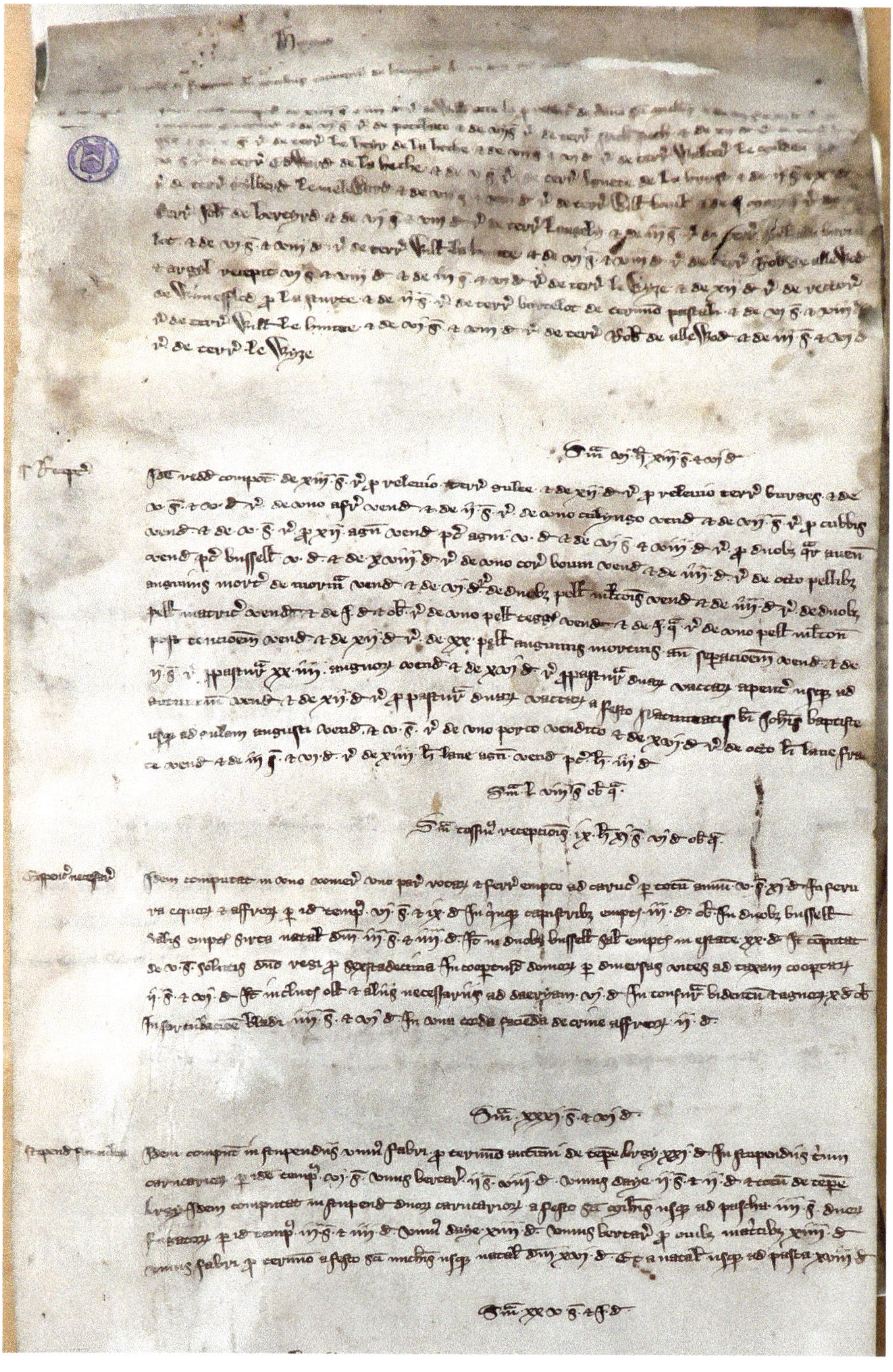

Fig. 20. Rental of Wintney Priory and Herriard Grange, 14th century. HRO, 44M69/E1/2/48.

and again in the years before 1365, then averaging 64 a. Nevertheless, by the end of the century it had recovered to 160 a.[275]

As elsewhere, the chalklands were characterised by large sheep flocks.[276] Here the priory maintained both a breeding and a wether flock. Until the 1420s, it consistently maintained a flock of 200 sheep (except in 1340, 1341 and 1365), and usually kept much more. It stocked most intensively in the period 1385–1405 averaging over 640 sheep and with a peak of 810 in 1393.[277] As elsewhere, in some years the wool was specifically sent to the estate headquarters to be combined for sale. Sheep were also integrated into wider estate policy. Thus in 1396/7 hoggasters were sent from Hartley and others sent to neighbouring Lasham, wethers were sent to Lasham, and lambs were sent from Hartley and then returned there later in the year after shearing.[278] The more substantial tenants of the main manor of Herriard also kept large flocks of their own. The freeholder Adam de la Lye had a sheepfold for 100 sheep c.1272,[279] and at the end of the century Robert of Dogemersfield was granted pasture over most of the parish for three years for 150 sheep and 200 ewes.[280]

Other livestock included horses, cattle, pigs and poultry. In 1335 the manor possessed eight horses, 20 oxen, four cows, ten young cattle, 11 pigs, and poultry.[281] Cows were kept both for breeding and, as with the ewes. for milk which could be made into cheese. Their numbers rose in the 1340s and 1350s, then fell in the 1360s before recovering at the end of the century. In 1387, 99 cheeses were produced, of which 40 went to the tenants as rewards at harvest or sheep washing, 26 were sold, 21 went to the cellarer of the priory, and ten were taken for tithes. The relative value of cattle and sheep milk for milk is reflected when they were leased, cows leased for 3s. and ewes between 1d. and 2d.[282] Cows were often leased for their milk as in 1339.[283] In 1404/5 eight cows and 112 sheep were leased for milking.[284]

As a relatively new lord, the priory would have lacked heavy tenant services, apart from certain specific tasks at harvest and sheep washing when all labour was required, for which they were rewarded with bread, ale, meat, fish, or cheese. The numbers involved declined in the course of the 14th century. For the most part the regular labour would have been provided by a group of *famuli* or farm servants: a ploughman, drivers, a carter, usually two shepherds, a swineherd, and a dairymaid although the number of such servants fell in 1350s, from about ten to about seven by the later 14th century.

275 Hare, 'Wintney Priory', tab. 2. HRO, 44/M69/1/3/4, mm. 4, 6
276 Hare, 'Bishop and the prior', 198–9, 203; idem, 'Hampshire agriculture in the Middle Ages', 70.
277 Hare, 'Wintney Priory', tab. 3.
278 HRO, 44M69/A1/3/6, m. 3.
279 HRO, 44M69/C5.
280 HRO, 44M69/C243.
281 HRO, 44M69/A1/3/4, m. 1.
282 HRO, 44M69/A1/3/4, m. 28.
283 HRO, 44M69/A1/3/4, m. 6.
284 HRO, 44M69/A1/3/6, m. 7.

Early Modern Farming (*c*.1550–1793)

An estimate of the late 16th century reckoned the total land in the parish amounted
to approximately 58 yardlands, of which the demesnes accounted for 24 yardlands.[285]
A survey of 1577 reckoned the demesnes to amount to 1,204 a., comprising 577
a. of arable land, 210 a. of pasture, 28 a. of meadow, 215 a. of heath, and 174 a of
woods.[286] The remaining land in the parish was divided between 18 estates, including
12 freehold estates. The largest of these was Lee farm, accounting for 7 yardlands,
followed by Herriard Grange at 5½ yardlands. Three other tenants held between 2
and 4 yardlands, and the remaining land was divided into 13 estates of 1 yardland
each.[287] A more thorough survey of 1604 detailed the 12 freehold estates. The largest
estate was Lee farm, held by Richard Lee and comprising 394 a., of which 288 a. were
in his hands and the remaining 106 a. were let to five tenants, each holding between
12 a. and 32 acres. Herriard Grange amounted to 247 a., of which 222 a. were let to
Richard Lee and the remainder was divided between two smallholdings. Three more
freeholders held estates of more than 100 a., five held estates of between 30 a. and 35

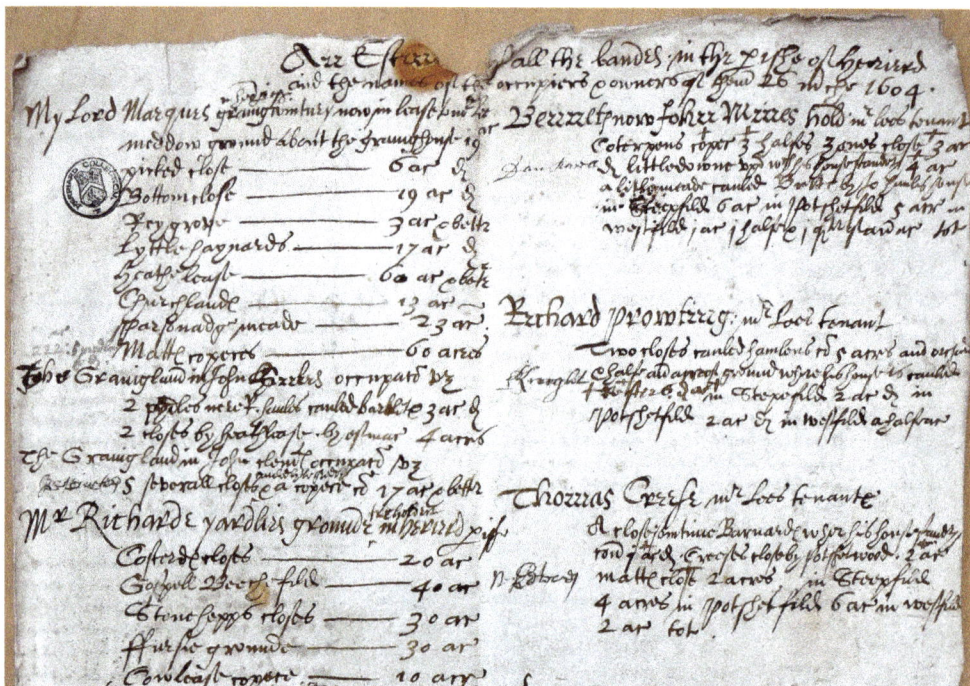

Fig. 21. Sir Richard Paulet's estimation of all the lands in Herriard, 1604. HRO, 44M69/E1/1/9.

285 HRO, 44M69/E1/1/13. It is stated in a survey of 1604 that the size of the yardland used
     here was 40 acres: HRO, 44M69/E1/1/9.
286 HRO, 44M69/E1/1/2–3.
287 HRO, 44M69/E1/1/13.

a., and there were two small tenements of only a few acres each.[288] The customary rents of the freeholders in 1583 amounted to £4 19s. 10d. and 1 lb of cumin a year. Nine more tenants held by leases for lives, paying rents totalling to £9 0s. 8d. a year.[289] After the exchange by Richard Paulet of land for a copyhold tenement in 1581 no further mention is made of copyholders, suggesting that customary tenure had been eliminated in favour of leasehold by the late 16th century.[290] By the late 17th century the parish was reckoned to amount to approximately 67 yardlands, divided between the demesnes (now said to be 30 yardlands) and 18 other estates. Lee farm was still the largest of these, estimated at 10 yardlands, whilst Herriard Grange still amounted to 5½ yardlands. Another holding measured 5 yardlands, and two more measured 3 yardlands each, whilst the remaining land was divided between 14 estates of 1 yardland or less.[291]

By the late 16th century, most of the demesne arable and pasture was let out in small parcels. Soon after his marriage to Lady Elizabeth Windsor, George Puttenham let the demesnes for 15 years, letting the mansion house with its gardens and orchards to the same tenant in the following year. Despite his bitter dispute with Elizabeth and her son John Paulet over his control of the manor, Puttenham let the manor and demesnes again for another 12 years in 1574.[292] After the privy council thwarted Puttenham's illegal attempt to sell the manor to his friend Sir John Throckmorton, despite only holding it in the right of his estranged wife,[293] John Paulet successfully sued Puttenham for waste and wrested most of the demesnes into his own hands.[294] The impact of Puttenham's tenure can be seen in the diminished value of the land in the years after he held the manor. A list of rents from 1580 records 12 parcels of the demesnes were let to 14 tenants for a total annual rent of £36 3s. 4d,[295] but the same lands had previously been let by Puttenham for sums totalling almost £68.[296] The whole value of the land let by Puttenham had amounted to £147.[297]

In 1583 Richard Paulet compiled a detailed list of the demesnes, calculating that after improvement they would be worth £200 a year.[298] At this date, a handful of tenants still owed the lord work and rents in kind. In 1597 two tenants of part of the demesnes owed a total of two week's work on the lord's land besides their rent, and

288 HRO, 44M69/E1/1/9.
289 HRO, 44M69/E1/1/2–3.
290 HRO, 44M69/D1/6/M33.
291 HRO, 44M69/E1/1/19. The document is undated, but refers to John Diggle, vicar of Herriard 1665–83.
292 HRO, 44M69/D1/6/A8, 11, 16; above, Landownership (Manor of Herriard).
293 HRO, 44M69/C712; 44M69/D1/6/A16; 44M69/D1/6/A19; 44M69/F3/1; *Acts of PC, 1575–7*, 148.
294 HRO, 44M69/E4/83.
295 HRO, 44M69/E1/1/1.
296 HRO, 44M69/E4/83.
297 HRO, 44M69/E4/83.
298 HRO, 44M69/E1/1/2–3.

another three tenants of the demesnes owed payments in wheat or barley.[299] These extra burdens appear to have been eliminated three years later, when demesne land worth a total value of £171 was divided between 24 tenants. More land, worth £108 a year, was still in Sir Richard Paulet's hands at that time.[300] Paulet's purchase of the wardship of Thomas Jervoise in 1601 necessitated an augmentation of the revenues of the manor,[301] and from that year the demesnes were let to 33 tenants paying a total of £260 a year.[302]

Lying on the Hampshire chalk downlands, Herriard's agriculture continued to be dominated by traditional sheep-corn farming. The principal crops throughout the early modern period were wheat, barley, and oats, supplemented by smaller amounts of rye, peas, and beans. A hopyard was also established to in the late 16th century, although hops were never a significant crop.[303] In the 1580s, Richard Paulet carefully calculated the cost and profits of all of his agricultural activities, both the rearing of livestock and the planting of crops. In a typical year, he anticipated that his team of eight horses would plough 170 a. of land. Of this, 90 a. would be sown with 30 quarters of wheat, 40 a. with 20 quarters of barley, and another 40 a. with 20 quarters of oats. He expected each year's harvest to produce four times as much grain as was sown, even after deductions for tithes, from which one quarter was to be set aside for the following year's crop. From the remainder of the harvest, Paulet calculated that his household would consume 6 bushels of wheat each week, or *c.*38 quarters a year. The same amount of barley would be used in malting, the horses, boars and stalled oxen would consume 4 bushels a week, or 26 quarters a year, of oats, and the poultry would consume half a peck a week, or 1 quarter a year, in oatmeal. Paulet allowed from each year's harvest another *c.*23 quarters of wheat, 15 quarters of barley and 15 quarters of oats for the provision of his husbandmen and draught animals. This would leave a surplus for the market each year of *c.*29 quarters of wheat, 7 quarters of barley, and 18 quarters of oats. Besides these staples, small quantities of other crops cultivated on the estate included hemp for harnesses, and vetches and peas to feed livestock. Two bushels of peas were also to be set aside to supplement the diet of the household during lent.[304]

In the five years between 1583–4 and 1587–8 there were sown on average each year approximately 27 quarters of wheat, 26 quarters of oats and 25 quarters of barley, but the actual amount could vary widely, particularly for oats. The amount of wheat sown each year ranged between 21 quarters and 32 quarters, and between 18 quarters and 34 quarters of barley, but oats ranged between 10 quarters and 69 quarters. In addition, in one year there were also sown 9 quarters of dredge, a mixture of oats

299 HRO, 44M69/E1/1/5.
300 HRO, 44M69/E1/1/7.
301 HRO, 44M69/F4/19/1.
302 HRO, 44M69/E1/1/8.
303 HRO, 44M69/E1/1/5; 44M69/E2/16.
304 HRO, 44M69/E4/2.

and barley. Rye was apparently only an occasional crop at Herriard; 5 quarters of rye were sown in 1585, but none is noted in the following years.[305] During this period Richard Paulet began improving formerly barren ground through the use of marl in order ultimately to convert it to arable land.[306] A portion of the warren was cleared and sown with wheat *c.*1587, although with little success at first.[307] Nevertheless, *c.*320 a. of waste ground at Chatterdens, Herriard Deane and the warren were converted to arable use and enclosed in the late 16th century following an agreement with the freeholders.[308] Another innovation practised early in the 17th century, and possibly earlier, appears to be the adoption of a five-year course in parts of the demesnes, with the sowing of peas, wheat and barley in successive years, followed by two years of fallow.[309] Paulet's motivation appears to have been to increase the value at which the land could be rented, rather than to increase his own arable production. In 1605, 15 quarters of wheat were sown in the summer and another 25 quarters in the winter, including 9 quarters belonging to tenants, as well as 26 quarters of barley and 26 quarters of oats.[310] In the year 1606–7, *c.*35 quarters of wheat and *c.*32 quarters of oats were sown in the winter months, supplemented by small amounts of vetches, while 25 quarters of barley was sown during the summer.[311]

The manor was plundered by soldiers of the Royalist garrison at Basing House in September 1642, who carried away most of the corn grown on the demesnes, which were said subsequently to have lain in waste until the fall of the garrison in 1645.[312] Jervoise calculated the value of the crops and cattle taken by the garrison to amount to £4,000, whilst the occupation of the demesne by the besieging forces was said to have cost him £3,000 in lost income. Writing perhaps at the end of the 1640s, he complained that the damage done to the ground was so great he was still not able to fully stock it, nor to find tenants to rent it from him. In all, with timber cut down and the damage to buildings in the manor, Jervoise put his total losses at Herriard during the Civil War at £7,900.[313]

The demand for wheat to supply the needs of the household remained relatively stable, at 36–40 quarters a year, while the amount sown each year varied between about 20 and 35 quarters a year. In the years immediately after the Restoration, wheat typically represented approximately a quarter and barley approximately a third of the total grain harvested, although the amount harvested between 1664 and 1669 ranged between 60 quarters and 105 quarters a year for wheat, and 90 quarters and 152 quarters a year for barley. The relatively constant amounts required for provisioning

305 HRO, 44M69/E4/2.
306 HRO, 44M69/E1/1/12; 44M69/E4/30/4.
307 HRO, 44M69/E8/2/1/3.
308 HRO, 44M69/F2/14/7–8; below, Livestock.
309 HRO, 44M69/E4/68.
310 HRO, 44M69/E4/2.
311 HRO, 44M69/E4/2.
312 TNA, C 22/414/27.
313 HRO, 44M69/E6/161; below, Forest Management.

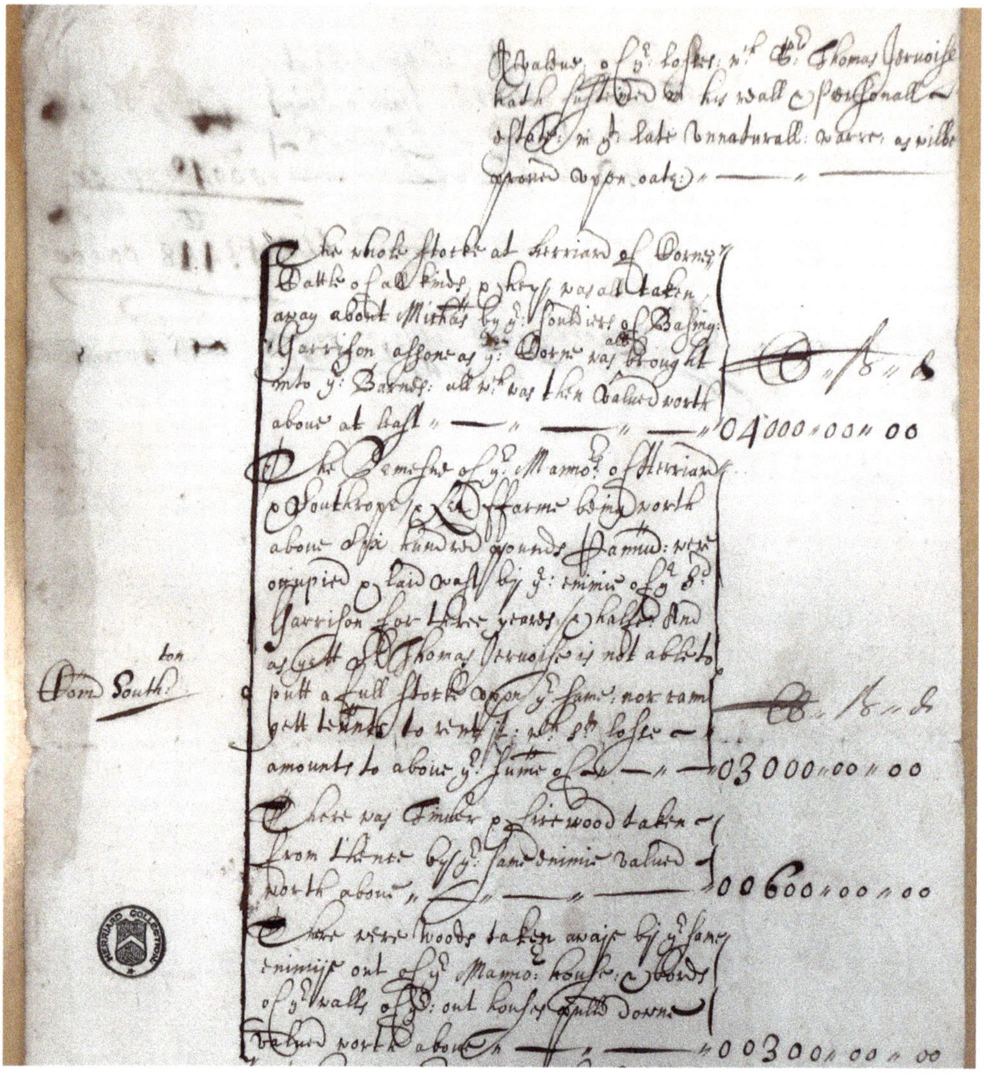
A Valew of ye losses wch Sr Thomas Jervoise hath susteyned in his reall & personall estate in ye late unnaturall warre, as will appeare upon oath —

The whole stocke at Herriard of Corne & Cattle of all kinds & hey was all taken away about Michas by ye souldiers of Basing Garrison as soone as ye Corne was brought into ye Barnes: all wch was then valued worth about at least — 04000 00 00

The Demesne of ye Mannors of Herriard & Southrope & ... farme being worth above six hundred pounds p annum: were occupied & laid wast by ye enimie of ye sd Garrison for three yeares & halfe And as Sr Thomas Jervoise is not able to putt a full stocke upon ye same: nor can gett tenants to rent it: wch sd losse amounts to above ye summe of — 03000 00 00

There was Timber & fire wood taken from thence by ye same enimie valued worth about — 00600 00 00

There were woods taken away by ye same enimies out of ye Mannor house & doores of ye walls of ye out houses pulled downe valued worth about — 00300 00 00

Corn South.

HERRIARD COLLECTION

Fig. 22. Sir Thomas (I) Jervoise's losses in the Civil War. HRO, 44M69/E6/161.

the household and for sowing the following year's harvest meant that the amount of corn remaining for the market varied with the annual yield. In 1664–5 the harvest of 105 quarters of wheat produced 44 quarters for the market, but the following year's yield of just 67 quarters left only 8 quarters for the market. Each year about 90 per cent of the barley harvested was set aside for malting, for the following year's harvest, or for sale, although the proportion in each category could vary from year to year. In 1665–6, when the harvest yielded only 90 quarters of wheat, almost half (43 quarters) was sown the following year, more than a third (33 quarters) was used for malting, and only 6 quarters was brought to market. In the following year, when 156 quarters of barley were harvested, 37 quarters were sown, 61 quarters were malted, and 52 quarters were sold. Oats and peas were the staple feed crops of the stock of the manor, and only occasionally were any excess amounts brought to market for sale, and never in large quantities.[314] New crops began to be introduced in the parish early in the 18th century, including sainfoin and teasels, the latter presumably for use in the cloth industry.[315]

Livestock

In the late 16th century it was claimed that only the freeholders and their tenants had any rights in the commons, following a longstanding arrangement whereby the lords of the manor had exchanged their rights in the commons in return for enclosing a portion of the common fields and taking it in hand.[316] This arrangement presumably dated from at least the middle of the 15th century, when the prioress of Wintney complained that her common rights in the parish had been withdrawn by the lord of the manor.[317] By the middle of the 16th century it was accepted that Herriard Grange had no common rights in the parish, despite the marquess of Winchester's failed attempt to common his cattle in the warren.[318] It was complained to lord keeper Sir John Puckering in the 1590s that Sir Richard Paulet had exchanged a copyhold tenement for demesne land of much greater value, in order to acquire pasture rights in the commons. The freeholders subsequently complained that he had put 200–300 sheep into the commons each year, more than they felt the commons could bear.[319] By this date, and probably much earlier, large parts of the common fields had been enclosed and were held separately. In the middle of the 16th century the stint (or allowance) for those with common grazing rights was to keep 100 sheep for every yardland held in the common fields, but their partial enclosure necessitated a renegotiation. During the 1580s it was agreed that the stint should be three sheep for every acre held in the common fields, or two sheep for every acre held of enclosed land, and six rother beasts (usually oxen) or horses for every yardland.[320] By 1623 the stint in the commons was six rother beasts, three horses, and 60 sheep for every yardland held, or the equivalent rate.[321] Commoners were not permitted to let any part of their stint to anybody without first having offered it to the tenants and freeholders of the manor.[322]

During the 16th century the sheep belonging to the lord of the manor were divided into three flocks, one of breeding ewes, one of lambs, and one of castrated wethers, the first two flocks tended by a separate shepherd from the latter. The wethers were usually kept in the commons, whilst the rams, ewes and lambs were

314 HRO, 44M69/E7/3.
315 HRO, Inventory of Hugh James, 1725B/040; Inventory of Henry Lewis, 1732AD/063.
316 HRO, 44M69/F2/14/7–8.
317 HRO, 44M69/F2/14/39.
318 HRO, 44M69/F2/14/7–8.
319 HRO, 44M69/F2/14/7–8.
320 HRO, 44M69/A1/3/1; 44M69/F2/14/8.
321 HRO, 44M69/A1/3/13.
322 HRO, 44M69/A1/3/13.

folded in the 'ingrounds', enclosed pasture closer to the demesne farm. During the 16th century stock from Herriard frequently passed between it and the Paulet manor of Freefolk, where Lady Anne Paulet kept a household.[323] The combined stock of the manors of Herriard and Weston Corbett were let to farmers in 1577, presumably before the Paulets had wrested control of the stock from Puttenham. The two manors together maintained more than 1,000 sheep and 300 lambs, 30 cows and one bull, eight oxen, and five horses, all of which were let, together with 116 a. of arable land to support them, for a rent of £100.[324] By the summer of 1587 the stock was firmly in the hands of Richard Paulet, who recorded that there were 579 sheep and 238 lambs on the manor, reduced by death and sales to 486 sheep and 198 lambs and tegs by the following winter.[325] In the summer of 1598 the flock of wethers on the common numbered 266, whilst there were 142 rams and ewes and 208 lambs grazing on the ingrounds, including 131 lambs bought that month at Farley and Ecchinswell, making a total of 616 sheep.[326] When the wethers and adults were sheared they produced 408 fleeces, amounting to 26 tods which, at 30 lb per tod, weighed more than 780 lb.[327] The flock produced over 31 tods of wool in the following year, and 26 tods in 1600.[328] In the winter of 1605 the flock was a similar size, numbering 627 sheep, including 168 tegs of that spring's birth.[329] By the summer of 1609 this number had increased to a total of 961 sheep on the manor, comprising 241 wethers on the common, and 501 sheep and 219 lambs in the ingrounds. Of these, 16 were sent to Freefolk for fattening and 121 were set aside for store, leaving 824 for the following year.[330] In the summer of 1639 there were 519 sheep and 191 lambs, which together produced over 32 tods of wool.[331] Despite the depredations of the Civil Wars, the flock at Herriard comprised 1,042 sheep in 1653, of which 228 were sold, slaughtered, or died of disease over the following 12 months. Nevertheless, the flock number 1,028 in October 1654, with 312 wethers, 450 ewes, 19 rams, 214 teggs, and 33 fattening sheep.[332]

The manor could also support large numbers of cattle and horses, many of which were let out for an annual rent, both to serve as draught animals and for their milk. In the year 1597–8, 63 cows and oxen were let to 26 individuals for a total of over £30 a year.[333] There were 74 head of cattle in the hands of the lord of the manor in 1599, comprising 20 cows, five oxen, two bulls, four fatting beasts, and 24 weanlings, or recently weaned calves; of these, the four fatting beasts, one bull and 12 weanlings

323 HRO, 44M69/E4/10.
324 HRO, 44M69/E1/1/60.
325 HRO, 44M69/E4/2.
326 HRO, 44M69/E4/14.
327 HRO, 44M69/E4/13.
328 HRO, 44M69/E4/18.
329 HRO, 44M69/E4/2.
330 HRO, 44M69/E4/6.
331 HRO, 44M69/E6/12/2.
332 HRO, 44M69/E6/13.
333 HRO, 44M69/E4/12.

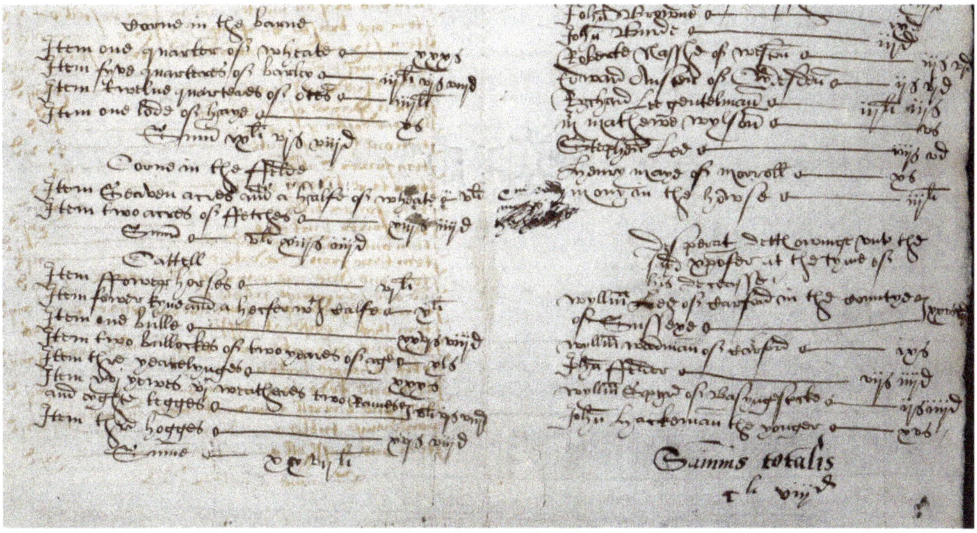

Fig. 23. Detail from the inventory of the blacksmith Christopher Willmott (d.1586), showing his crops and cattle. HRO, 1586A/94.

were sent to provision Lady Paulet's household at Freefolk later that year. Besides these, there were a number of manorial stock let to tenants. One tenant, John Hockley, rented four oxen and four cows from the manor, for a total of £22, as well as 40 sheep and 40 lambs, for another £18, and two mares, for £6. Another 34 cows were let to 12 demesnes tenants, for a total of £88, and six oxen and 13 cows were rented to foreigners for £59. There were 18 horses, including colts, stocked on the lord's lands, and two more were let to Hockley for £6.[334]

The ready access to pasture in the parish is reflected in the large amounts of cattle and sheep recorded in the extant probate records of the 16th and 17th centuries. Of a total of 49 extant probate inventories from the parish dating from between 1549 and 1732, 44 recorded possession of some livestock. Of these, 39 had at least one cow or ox (including two with no sheep), and 35 had sheep (including four without any cattle). Although not every inventory recorded a figure for the number of cattle or the amount of sheep, the amount of livestock held by each individual ranged widely, varying between one and 20 cows, and two and 280 sheep per person. Excluding those who had none, there were on average five cows and 54 sheep per individual. The inventories suggest that the abundant commons and pasture within the parish enabled even relatively humble parishioners to keep large amounts of livestock. Of the 34 inventories from before the Civil War, 17 were valued at less than £20, including six worth under £10. Twelve of these 17 inventories recorded cows, including three with three or more cows, and 13 recorded sheep, including ten with ten or more sheep, of whom five parishioners had at least 20 sheep and one had over 50 sheep. Of the six parishioners whose possessions were valued at less than £10, four had at least

334 HRO, 44M69/E4/16.

one cow and the same number had at least one sheep, including one who had more than 20 sheep and two had ten sheep or more. Only four of the 15 inventories proved after the Restoration were valued at under £20, but of these two recorded three cows or more, and two recorded at least one sheep, including one with ten sheep or more.

Even those with little or no land could keep several beasts. Nine of the 49 inventories from the parish recorded possession of livestock with no reference to land or crops in a barn. If the inventory of Elizabeth Hall is excluded, whose six head of cattle and 49 sheep amounted at £28 to more than a third of the total value of her inventory, the other eight inventories that recorded livestock and no land or crops were all worth less than £20, including four worth less than £10. Two of these, the vicar Lewis Thomas (d. 1584) and William Simes (d. 1728), kept no cattle or sheep and only a couple of pigs, although the vicar also kept a horse worth £4, as befitted his status.[335] Of the remaining six, all kept at least one head of cattle, and all but one also kept sheep. Lawrence Wilkins had one cow and 40 sheep when he died in 1562, and Richard Elkins had four head of cattle and 21 sheep in 1594.[336] Several more parishioners with only small quantities of land sown with crops or harvested grain in store also kept large numbers of livestock. Thomas Clement had 2½ a. sown with wheat and two cows and 56 sheep; Richard Barling held 1½ a. sown with oats, together with 37 sheep and lambs; John Wareham, who had 2 a. sown with wheat and vetches, owned eight head of cattle and 20 sheep; Robert Rivers had 1 a. of wheat and 10 sheep.[337] The goods of Nicholas Lipscombe, proved in 1601, included only small quantities of grain, comprising one quarter of barley, 6 bushels of malt and 12 bushels of oats, with four cows and 73 sheep.[338]

At the other end of the social spectrum, eight inventories were valued at £100 or more, including six worth at least £200. One of these, the spinster Elizabeth Hyde, left no stock amongst her possessions.[339] Of the remaining seven wealthy parishioners, at least six held three head of cattle or more, including three with at least ten head of cattle. The widow Mary Dallman of Herriard Grange left 13 head of cattle when she died in 1705,[340] and her son Ambrose left 20 when he died two years later.[341] Although the inventory of Nathaniel Hyde, proved in 1675, did not record the number of cattle kept on his farm, at a value of £51 the herd must have been of a significant size, far exceeding the value even of Ambrose Dallman's 20 head of cattle, which had been

335 HRO, Inventory of Lewis Thomas, 1584B/086; Inventory of William Simes, 1728A/110.
336 HRO, Inventory of Lawrence Wilkins, 1562A/064; Inventory of Richard Elkins, 1594A/039.
337 HRO, Inventory of Thomas Clement, 1578B/025; Inventory of Richard Barling, 1584B/005; Inventory of John Wareham, 1586A/086; Inventory of Robert Rivers, 1664A/080.
338 HRO, Inventory of Nicholas Lipscombe, 1601A/049.
339 HRO, Inventory of Elizabeth Hyde, 1678AD/062.
340 HRO, Inventory of Mary Dallman, 1705A/025.
341 HRO, Inventory of Ambrose Dallman, 1707AD/058.

priced at £35.[342] These wealthy parishioners kept large numbers of sheep, with the four for whom a figure was recorded owning between 115 and 280 sheep, an average of 195 sheep. Of the three remaining inventories for which no number of sheep was recorded, all had between £45 and £61 of sheep, suggesting between 150 and 300 sheep each.[343]

Despite the large number of cattle in the parish, there is little evidence of dairying for the market. Few inventories record large amounts of cheese or butter, with only three inventories recording significant quantities of either. William Hayes' 37 cheese in 1603 were valued at £1, in the same year John Hale left an unspecified quantity of butter and cheese, together worth £1 10s., and in 1675 Nathaniel Hyde's 300 cheeses were valued at £5 13s. 6d.[344] The large quantity of beef and bacon, worth over £14, left by Mary Dallman in 1705 is presumably evidence of the size of her household at Herriard Grange rather than meat produced for the market.[345] Two parishioners also kept bees.[346]

Agriculture since 1793

From the late 17th century there was a tendency towards dividing most of the demesne land between a handful of large farms. The first of these was Manor or West farm, known initially as 'Taplins' after its first tenant, established in 1677 with a substantial new farmhouse and 360 a. of land.[347] East farm was established 20 years later.[348] In 1793 West farm, East farm, and Lee farm comprised between 300 and 400 a. each, three more farms comprised between 150 a. and 200 a. each, and another four estates amounted to under 100 a., including two less than 20 a. in size.[349] In the same year, George Purefoy Jervoise calculated the demesnes to amount to 139 a., comprising 55 a. of arable, 35 a. of meadow, 39 a. of pasture, and almost 9 a. of gardens surrounding the house.[350] Of this, 49 a. of arable was intended to be converted into pasture in 1793, and the remainder into a coppice.[351]

By the late 18th century the Jervoise family were no longer keeping large numbers of sheep permanently on the manor, instead purchasing sheep to fatten up before selling them again at a profit. In 1793–4 63 wether sheep were purchased, including

342 HRO, Inventory of Nathaniel Hide, 1675A/051.
343 HRO, Inventory of Nathaniel Hide, 1675A/051; Inventory of Mary Dallman, 1705A/025; Inventory of Henry Lewis, 1732AD/063.
344 HRO, Inventory of William Hayes, 1603AD/027; Inventory of John Hale, 1603B/024; Inventory of Nathaniel Hide, 1675A/051.
345 HRO, Inventory of Mary Dallman, 1705A/025.
346 HRO, Inventory of Thomas Clement, 1578B/025; Inventory of John Hale, 1603B/024.
347 HRO, 44M69/D1/6/H1–2; 44M69/E7/17.
348 HRO, 44M69/D1/6/M48; 44M69/E2/52.
349 HRO, 44M69/E1/1/37.
350 HRO, 44M69/E13/1/1.
351 HRO, 44M69/E1/1/43.

Fig. 24. Park Farm. © Barbara Large.

30 at Britford (Wilts.), for a total value of £62. In the same period, the flock produced 3 tods and 17 lb of wool, worth over £4, and sold 62 wether sheep for a total of £88. In 1797 Jervoise purchased 60 sheep, all of which he sold for a profit of just £6, which may explain why he did not purchase sheep in the following years. Two years later Jervoise sold ten oxen, a cow and a calf for £163, whilst beef, milk and butter raised another £20. Rents for cattle grazing raised another £47, and hay for stabling another £57, which left profits of over £180. Even greater profits were achieved in 1800, when 45 tonnes of hay was sold for £284.[352] An inventory of the stock belonging to Jervoise in 1816 recorded one bull, ten cows and two calves, 199 wether sheep, ten ewes, seven lambs and one ram; four ewes and four lambs were Merino sheep, the rest South Down. The wool of 205 South Down sheep had produced 20 tods of wool, worth £40, and five merino ewes another 20 lb of wool, worth £4. Besides the sheep and cattle, 120 tonnes of meadow grass, 12 tonnes of clover and 4 tonnes of sainfoin were together worth £666.[353]

Writing in 1838, the tithe commissioner remarked upon the widely differing quality of soil within the parish, although he found the clay not as stiff there as that found to the north of Basingstoke. Despite observing a lack of any particular examples of 'high farming' he thought the land well cultivated, also noting the 'true enterprising sprit prevailing amongst the farmers' in the parish. There were at that time 1,343 a. of arable land, of which one-quarter was sown with wheat, one-quarter with oats,

352 HRO, 44M69/E13/1/1.
353 HRO, 44M69/E13/1/23.

one-quarter with seeds, and the remainder lay fallow. Another 736 a. were meadow land, of which 200 a. was mown and the rest grazed upon, and there were 424 a. of woodland. The commons then measured 257 a.[354] By that time, East farm had been taken back in hand and its land thrown into the park, which now occupied a quarter of the parish. George Purefoy Jervoise then held a total of 842 a. in hand, comprising 510 a. of woodland, 179 a. of common and 139 a. of pasture, with no arable land. Most of the rest of the Jervoise land in the parish was divided between two large farms, West farm (606 a.) and Lee farm (570 a.), and two medium-sized farms, Hydes farm (237 a.) and Hale farm (153 a.). Lord Bolton's land was divided between Grange farm, measuring 138 a., another 69 a. let to his kinsman Revd John Orde, the rector of Winslade, 67 a. remaining in his own hands, and 23 a. let to the tenant of West farm. Of the remaining small freeholds only three – Botilds farm (57 a.), Lipscombe farm (41 a.), and Richard Wise's farm (28 a.) – were larger than 20 a. Four smallholdings measured less than 20 a., combining a mix of freehold and leasehold land.[355] During the second half of the 19th century the Jervoise family purchased most of the parish not already in their possession. The most substantial of these acquisitions was Herriard Grange, purchased from the trustees of the Bolton estates in 1851.[356] Botilds farm, amounting to 56 a., had preceded it in 1849,[357] and Hale farm and Lipscombe farm both followed in 1855.[358] Several smaller estates were added in the later part of the century.[359]

By the late 19th century the wheat, oats, and fodder crops dominated arable land use in Herriard. Land farmed in the parish in 1867 was sown with wheat (40s a.), oats (292 a.), cabbage, kohl raby and rape (360 a.), turnips (283 a.), and vetches (131 a.), with smaller quantities of barley (55 a.), peas (23 a.), mangold (12 a.), potatoes (1 a.). Another 338 a. lay under clover, 94 a. lay fallow, and there were 762 a. of permanent pasture land in the parish, providing grazing for 86 head of cattle, 2,602 sheep and lambs, and 245 pigs.[360] At the same time, the estate was investing in agricultural improvement, for instance through the employment of agricultural engines by 1881, to which had been added a traction engine by 1891.[361] Towards the end of the century, there appears to have been an increased focus upon dairying in the parish. Home farm was stocked with shorthorn dairy cattle in 1883.[362] Until the 1890s, milk produced in the parish was taken to London by train from Basingstoke, but a modern cheese-making dairy was established at Manor farm in 1892, with the intention of

354 TNA, IR 18/9021.
355 HRO, 21M65/F7/115/1–2.
356 HRO, 44M69/D1/6/K1; 44M69/D1/6/M3; above, Landownership (Wintney Herriard Grange).
357 HRO, 44M69/D1/6/M18.
358 HRO, 44M69/D1/6/M4; 44M69/D1/6/M19.
359 HRO, 44M69/D1/6/M5–19.
360 TNA, MAF 68/128/3.
361 Census, 1881; 1891.
362 *Hants. Chron.* 1 Sep. 1883.

converting the farm's excess milk into cheese.[363] This change of focus presumably explains the dramatic shift in land use by 1899, with a fall in the amount of arable to 754 a., less than half the land sown with crops as there had been in 1867, and an increase of pasture to a total of 1,543 a. There had been a fourfold increase in the number of cattle kept in the parish since 1867, to a total of 324 head of cattle, whilst sheep farming was significantly in decline, with a total of 420 in the parish. There were also less than half the number of pigs, 114 in total, than there had been in 1867. Wheat (219 a.) and oats (201 a.) remained the two principal corn crops, with smaller amounts of peas (18 a.), barley (16 a.) and rye (5 a.). There had been a significant reduction in the amount of fodder crops cultivated, with only turnips (130 a.), vetches (26 a.) and mangold (19 a.) measuring more than 10 acres.[364]

By 1925 there were ten farms or smallholdings in total, of which two were larger than 300 a. each, four more measured between 150 a. and 300 a., and the remaining four were all less than 50 a. each, including one with less than 5 a. Together, these holdings provided regular employment for 33 men and 16 boys, and casual work for one man and three women. By this date, there had been a further reduction in the amount of arable and pasture, of c.100 a. each, suggesting that both were being converted to rough grazing or woodlands. This supported 363 head of cattle and 576 sheep and lambs, although there had been a fall in the number of pigs to 46. Wheat (171 a.) and oats (176 a.) remained the two main corn crops, with 75 a. of barley and 3 a. of rye. As well as turnips (60 a.), vetches (40 a.), cabbages and rape (22 a.), mangold (21 a.), and potatoes (1 a.), there were 23 a. of mustard growing for seed. An acre of orchard was planted with apple, pear, cherry and plum trees.[365]

During the Second World War there were nine farms and holdings in the parish, three were larger than 300 a., two were between 150 a. and 300 a., and three were between 50 a. and 150 a., and one small holding had less than 20 a. All of the holdings engaged in mixed farming to a greater or lesser extent, but only on three of the largest farms was there a significant amount of arable land. At least two-fifths of the land of each of Manor farm (544 a.), Lee farm (334 a.), and Hydes farm (298 a.) were sown with corn crops, together representing almost three-quarters of all of the arable land in 1943. Wheat (310 a.) and oats (255 a.) remained the principal crops, with smaller amounts of mixed grain (71 a.), barley (30 a.), rye (13 a.) and beans (3 a.). Besides small quantities of root vegetables and fodder crops, the remaining arable crops included 8 a. of flax and 4 a. of maize at Manor farm, and 7 a. of mustard at Lee farm. There were by this time 490 head of cattle in the parish, with all but the smallholding having at least 30 head of cattle, and the four largest farms each having between 60 and 90 head of cattle. By comparison there were very few sheep or pigs, with the 202 sheep at Home farm the only sizeable flock, and a total of 26 pigs kept in the parish. Lee farm had 1,200 poultry birds, and Hydes farm almost 500, whilst

363 *Hants. & Berks. Gaz.* 3 Sep. 1892.
364 TNA, MFA 68/1781/14.
365 TNA, MAF 68/3242/4.

both Manor farm and Park farm had 200 poultry birds or more. The farms provided regular employment for 16 men, four boys and two women, and casual employment for one more boy. Only two of the farmers in the parish were rated as Grade A by the Ministry of Agriculture, with others criticised for lack of experience, lack of capital, or laziness.[366]

Since the 1940s there has been a process of amalgamation and specialisation. Until the 1980s there were three commercial dairies, each with over 100 head of cattle, and five mainly arable units, with over 600 sheep and 80 beef cattle across the estate. In 2025 there are three main farms. Park farm is a dairy farm occupying 600 a., half sown with wheat and maise, and the remainder providing grassland for a *c.*240-head herd of pedigree Holstein milking cows, with another *c.*260 head of young cattle. Manor farm is farmed in-hand primarily as an arable farm of just over 1100 a., growing wheat and maize. Hydes farm is entirely arable, with the addition of free-range chickens. Across the three farms there are about 200 ewes with lambs and 80 head of cattle. Produce is sold from a farm shop, and there are vegetable and flower market gardens.[367]

Woodland management

THE PARISH HAS probably always been heavily wooded,[368] and wood and timber would have represented a valuable resource for the lords of the manors. Despite this Domesday Book made only passing reference to it, recording that there was woodland for enclosing (*ad clausura*) without giving any indication of its quantity or value.[369] The manor of Herriard was said in 1366 to contain 100 a. of woodland.[370] Hen Wood has probably always been cultivated as coppices, and the wood growing in the western portion of the wood was sold in 1390 to one Hugo Barkescale of Basingstoke for 12*s.*[371]

Medieval deeds attest to the possession of several parcels of woodland by some of the tenants in Herriard, smaller than the demesne woodlands, but which would nevertheless have represented valuable resources to their owners.[372] Woodlands referred to in the 13th century include *Botildeswode*, which stood between the park and a field called *la Rude*,[373] and woods belonging to the Bovile, Lee and Herriard

366 TNA, MAF 32/980/68.
367 'Joe Ives describes the advantages of his robotic milking system', *Bright Maize*, https://www.brightmaize.com/joe-ives-describes-advantages-robotic-milking-system (accessed 4 Mar. 2025) ; info. from Mr J. Jervoise, 2025.
368 Above, Agricultural Landscape.
369 *Domesday*, 108.
370 HRO, 44M69/C276.
371 HRO, 44M69/C194.
372 HRO, 44M69/C341; 44M69/C351; 44M69/C353; 44M69/C362.
373 HRO, 44M69/C341.

families.[374] *Inglaisewode*, referred to in the middle of the 14th century, was named for the Ingelay family of the previous century.[375] Early in the 15th century a grove of wood called *Pottersgrove*, the former possession of the Fuges family, was granted to William Luyde,[376] whose descendants held it still in the 16th century.[377] Matts Copse, comprising 60 a. on the common, also occurs from the 16th century,[378] but presumably refers to the woodland held by William le Math in the 13th century.[379]

Accounts from the late 16th century onwards reveal the value of woodland resources to the lords of the manor. Hen Wood was said to measure 100 a. in 1577, when it was let to a tenant 'for the hedging',[380] whilst in 1583 the demesne underwood was said to measure 178 a.[381] Sales of underwood and timber from Hen Wood were worth a total of *c*.£33 a year in both 1582 and 1583. In the following year wood worth a total of *c*.£27 was sold on the manor, comprising underwood from Hen Wood, timber from Forfields and the Warren, bundles of firewood, and ash purchased by ash-burners and shovel makers.[382] The sale of hedge wood, worth less than other forms of wood, nevertheless raised more than £3 in 1590.[383] The amount of coppiced wood set aside for sale varied from year to year. A total of 10½ a. of coppiced wood was sold from Hen Wood in 1598 raising a total of *c*.£25, whilst another 2½ a. of coppiced wood in Honeyleaze Coppice was sold for almost £6, with small amounts also received for ash purchased by a wheelwright, and for hedge wood.[384] Two early 17th century surveys estimated that the woodland belonging to the demesne amounted to 215 a.,[385] whilst there was also a total of 142 a. of coppice and woodland in the hands of freeholders and their tenants.[386] The value of woodland resources remained relatively stable during the first half of the 17th century, with sales of coppice wood, firewood, poles and bark worth £39 in 1622, and £36 in the year 1624.[387] The wood from 6 a. of coppices, with poles, bark and other wood, raised more than £45 in 1639.[388] Underwood such as this continued to represent the bulk of the wood sold on the manor, but occasional sales of large amounts of timber could generate large profits, such as the 200 oaks felled in Hen Wood and 50 in Honeyleaze Coppice in 1634, sold for £180.[389] Amongst the losses he incurred

374 HRO, 44M69/C318; 44M69/C351; 44M69/C353; 44M69/C362; 44M69/C686.
375 HRO, 44M69/C90; 44M69/C114–5; 44M69/C319; 44M69/C323; 44M69/C340.
376 HRO, 44M69/C438.
377 HRO, 44M69/D1/6/M25–28.
378 HRO, 44M69/F2/14/23; 44M69/P1/106.
379 HRO, 44M69/C26; 44M69/C353.
380 HRO, 44M69/E1/1/60.
381 HRO, 44M69/E1/1/2.
382 HRO, 44M69/E4/1.
383 HRO, 44M69/E4/5.
384 HRO, 44M69/E4/15.
385 HRO, 44M69/E1/1/15.
386 HRO, 44M69/E1/1/9.
387 HRO, 44M69/E6/167.
388 HRO, 44M69/E6/15.
389 HRO, 44M69/E6/14.

Fig. 25. Section of a 17th-century plan, showing woods and heaths in the south of parish. HRO, 44M69/P/106.

during the Civil War, Jervoise calculated that timber and firewood worth £600 was taken by soldiers during the long siege of Basing House, with another £300 of damages done to the houses and outhouses of the manor by the removal of wooden boards.[390] Any damages incurred during the 1640s were apparently not long-lasting, with sales of 'coppice stuff' from Hen Wood worth £39 in 1655, and £70 in 1657.[391]

The felling of 820 timber trees in 1700, comprising 428 ash, 376 oaks and six beech trees, reveals the principal species of timber trees at that time.[392] From the year 1722, large numbers of trees were planted each year across the parish, numbering more than 3,300 in 1722, over 1,300 in 1723, and more than 2,700 in 1724, including 499 planted along the parish boundary at Herriard common, and over 4,000 in 1725. Of the species planted during these years, ash dominated, comprising two-thirds or more

390 HRO, 44M69/E6/161.
391 HRO, 44M69/E7/1.
392 HRO, 44M69/E8/2/6.

of the trees planted in each year. Other species planted at Herriard in the early 18th century included traditional standards, such as beech, elm, and oak, as well as horse chestnut, lime, silver fir, and spruce fir.[393] In 1770 Hen Wood was divided into 20 sections, ranging in size between 1 a. and 25 a., the oldest wood not having been cut since 1727. Six small compartments, measuring between 1 a. and 2 a., were set aside for the provision of wood to the tenants, with the wood from one of the six being cut each year in rotation.[394] When a survey was made in 1773 of the timber trees on Herriard common, there was found to be a total of almost 4,500 trees there, all of which were said to have been planted in the years 1723–40.[395]

From the late 18th century onwards, the Herriard woodlands were managed together with those at Tunworth and Lasham, so it is not always possible to distinguish Herriard from its neighbours. The coppice-with-standards system was introduced into northern Hampshire in the early 18th century, but it appears not to have been adopted at Herriard until much later in the century.[396] Until then, timber and coppice wood had been grown separately, particularly where the timber was beech. In 1794 the close at Lower Cowdreys was cleared before being planted with 8,000 ash trees and two bushels of hazel nuts, the only clear record of the adoption of coppice-with-standards in the parish, although a century later Francis H.T. Jervoise remarked on the widespread nature of the system throughout the parish.[397] Revenues from the estate's woodlands steadily rose across the final decade of the 18th century. In 1792 a total of £245 was raised from the sale of timber and coppice wood, although much of the latter was growing in Tunworth. Of the 25 a. of coppice wood sold that year, only 11 a. were growing in Herriard, although it was of greater value than the wood growing in Tunworth, raising £116 of the £205 total. To this was added another £40 for timber from an ash plantation.[398] The following year's sales represented a significant increase in revenue, with total sales worth £548. This revenue comprised £119 from the sale of ash, oak and fir timber, £248 for 22 a. of coppice wood, £131 for 80 loads of bark, and £50 for poles and faggots of wood.[399] Trees felled on the estate in 1794 included 396 oaks standing in Herriard and Tunworth, worth £470, and ash, elm and fir, worth £101, whilst c.26 a. of coppice were sold for £198, an annual revenue of £769. Another 49 oaks were felled in Herriard and Tunworth that year for Jervoise's own household's use.[400] The value of wood sold in 1795 exceeded £1,000, two-thirds of which was paid

---

393 HRO, 44M69/E6/167.
394 HRO, 44M69/P1/109.
395 HRO, 44M69/E11/101.
396 A. Albery, 'Woodland Management in Hampshire, 900 to 1815', *Rural History,* 22 (2011), 171–2; idem, unpubl. history of Herriard woods (I am grateful to Mr. J. Jervoise for providing me with a copy of this article).
397 HRO, 44M69E1/1/56.
398 HRO, 44M69/E13/5/2/1.
399 HRO, 44M69/E13/5/2/2.
400 HRO, 44M69/E13/5/3/1–2.

for the timber of 710 oak trees. Ash, elms, and two chestnut trees were also felled.[401] The revenues from the estate's woodlands exceeded £1,000 again in 1796, when oaks, ash, elms, and beech were felled.[402]

From the end of the 18th century an increasing diversification of tree species is also apparent, reflecting the maturing of the new species planted in the park and on the commons earlier in the century. Over the 1790s sales of fir timber gradually became more significant, raising £83 in 1797.[403] The annual timber auction of 1810 included not only the usual ash and beech trees, but also 32 walnut trees standing in various locations in Herriard, sold for a total of £195.[404] Sales of timber in 1819 included small numbers of lime trees.[405] The tithe award of 1840 revealed the extent to which the valuable woodlands of the parish remained almost an exclusive preserve of the two principal landowners. Of a total of almost 650 a. of woodland or plantations in the parish, 510 a. was kept in hand by the Jervoise family, whilst Lord Bolton owned another 85 a. Some 400 a. were growing in coppices or plantations of 10 a. or larger in area, of which the largest was still Hen Wood at 180 a. Another 66 a. of woodland were growing in rows between the fields, distributed across the parish and each measuring less than 2 a. in area.[406] The woodland of Herriard remained a valuable resource late in the 19th century. In the first five years of the 1880s sales of wood grown on the Herriard estate, which still included some woodlands in neighbouring parishes, ranged in value between a low of £636 in 1883–4 and a peak of £1,365 in 1884–5. Oak, beech and ash still predominated, with smaller amounts of elm, and an occasional tree of another species, including horse chestnut and sycamore.[407]

A detailed view of the state of woodlands in the parish early in the 20th century is provided by a survey undertaken by Francis H.T. Jervoise in advance of the introduction of a new scheme for the estate. At that time the existing forest growth was described as consisting mostly of hazel coppice interspersed with standards of oak and ash, except in a few places which were dominated instead by beech. Smaller amounts of larch and silver fir were also identified, and all five of these species were to be continued in the future, with the addition of spruce in a few places. Besides neglect, the survey identified rabbits and weeds, in particular blackthorn spreading from the hedgerows, as the two principal threats to the estate's profits. In order to achieve a fixed and sustainable annual income, it was proposed that the shelterwood compartment system be adopted for the regeneration and improvement of the estate's woodlands, by which the young crop is nurtured and grown under the shelter of existing adult trees.[408] Presumably under this

401 HRO, 44M69/E13/5/4/1–2.
402 HRO, 44M69/E13/5/5.
403 HRO, 44M69/E13/5/6–7.
404 HRO, 44M69/E13/5/19.
405 HRO, 44M69/E13/5/28.
406 HRO, 21M65/F7/115/1.
407 HRO, 44M69/E14/2.
408 HRO, 44M69/E1/1/56.

scheme, a large new plantation, comprising *c*.27 a., was laid out in the first decade of the 20th century at Forfield in the north of the parish.[409]

In 1904–5 sales of the estate's timber raised £650 and underwood another £144, contributing towards total revenues worth £890, although expenses of £371 reduced the profits to £519.[410] Sales of wood for the Herriard estate were worth a total of £885 in 1915–6, including £629 for the sale of oak, ash, beech and elm timber, and £102 for the sale of underwood. Against this must be set total costs of £458, reducing the profits from the estate's woodlands in that year to £427.[411] Revenues from the estate's woodlands had greatly increased by the middle of the century. Sales of timber in early 1948 raised a total of £1,146, although only 55 of the oak trees felled, worth £219, were grown in Herriard. The underwood sold in late 1947 was worth a total of £519, whilst the sale of firewood, poles, hurdles and other bundles of wood was also of significant value to the estate. The total value of wood sold or supplied to the use of the estate amounted in total to £3,950 in 1947–8. Besides ash, beech, and oak, other species grown commercially on the estate included cedar, chestnut, Douglas fir, larch, Scots pine, silver fir, and spruce.[412] By the later years of the century declining demand for wood impacted Herriard, and from 1965 J.L. Jervoise started a program of renewal. During the 1960s and 1970s some former sheep walks and field edges were cleared, returning c.70 a. to agriculture. Elsewhere, plantation sizes were increased to 10–20 a. each, where possible. There remained over 400 a. of hazel coppices with no commercial market, nearly half of which has been converted to a mixture of softwood and hardwood plantations. About 100 a. of coppice remain in rotation, supported by grants, to maintain the ecology and biodiversity, and the remainder is being gradually converted to mixed deciduous woodland.[413]

The Cloth Industry

LIKE NEIGHBOURING PARISHES, the proximity of Herriard to Basingstoke, a centre of the cloth trade of growing importance from the 15th century onwards, encouraged parishioners to combine agriculture with labouring in the cloth industry.[414] The earliest traces of the cloth industry in Herriard derive from probate industries from the middle of the 16th century. The possessions of William Hyde when he died in 1549 included significant amounts of crops in hand, cows, sheep and pigs, and a spinning wheel.[415] In the following decade Thomas Bowell alias Cox combined mixed farming with industry,

409 OS Map 1:2500, Hants. XXVI.4 (1910 edn).
410 HRO, 44M69/E17/8, pp. 73–8.
411 HRO, 44M69/E17/19.
412 HRO, 44M69/E17/5, ff. 10–26.
413 Info. from Mr J. Jervoise, 2025.
414 *Medieval Basingstoke.*
415 HRO, Will and inventory of William Hyde, 1549U/33.

owning crops, livestock, two wheels and a pair of cards.[416] In 1578 Thomas Clement had a wheel and a reel, and ½ tod of wool in his possession, besides 2½ a. of wheat in the ground, two cows and 56 sheep.[417] The labourer Richard Barling (d. 1584) had a small quantity of oats sown, presumably to sustain his 22 sheep, and owned a wheel, cards and a pair of shears. More than half of the value of his inventory was in the form of small debts owed to him by neighbours and relations, suggesting he also played an important role in local credit networks.[418]

Unsurprisingly, with so many sheep kept in the parish, there were also numerous references to wool or yarn in the probate inventories. In total, 14 of the 49 inventories refer to wool, ranging from 2 lb of wool and 6 lb of coarse wool, worth a total of 5*s.*, in the possession of the labourer John Fry in 1626,[419] to the yeoman Henry Lewis' stock of wool worth £8. John Hale had over 3 tods of wool (*c.*90 lb), worth £4, and Lawrence Wilkins left 32 fleeces, weighing one tod and three nails (*c.*50 lb) and valued at £1 11*s.*[420] Wilkins also had 20 lb of yarn, worth 15*s.*, whilst John Wise had 4 yd. of russet cloth, worth 5*s.*,[421] and John Fielder had a total of 12 yd. of cloth, in three different colours, worth £1 12*s.* 8*d.*[422] The decline of the cloth industry in north Hampshire during the late 17th century is reflected in the lack of evidence for it in the inventories of Herriard, with just one reference to it after 1650. Richard Page combined farming a smallholding with a handful of livestock and spinning, owning two wheels at the time of his death in 1682.[423]

Other Industries and Crafts

WHILST MOST PARISHIONERS before the 20th century were engaged in agricultural occupations, there is ample evidence of individuals employed in traditional rural crafts, including blacksmiths,[424] carpenters,[425] cordwainers,[426] tailors,[427] and wheelwrights.[428]

416 HRO, Will and inventory of Thomas Bowell alias Cox, 1557U/046.
417 HRO, Will and inventory of Thomas Clement, 1578B/025.
418 HRO, Will and inventory of Richard Barling, 1584B/05.
419 HRO, Inventory of John Fry, 1626AD/053.
420 HRO, Will and inventory of John Hale, 1603B/024.
421 HRO, Will and inventory of John Wise, 1570B/195.
422 HRO, Inventory of John Fielder, 1625AD/048.
423 HRO, Inventory of Richard Paige, 1682AD/064.
424 HRO, Will and inventory of Christopher Willmott, 1586A/94; Will and inventory of John Rampton, 1734A/098.
425 HRO, 21M65/E13/1798; 44M69/D1/6/D1; 44M69/E2/3; 44M69/E2/6; 44M69/E2/19; Will of Alice Knight, 1686B/27.
426 HRO, 44M69/G3/394; Administration of William Freeborn, 1803AD/18.
427 HRO, 44M69/E2/30; 44M69/F2/14/17.
428 HRO, 12M49/A37/3; Will and inventory of Thomas Saunder alias Wareham, 1592B/61; Administration of Henry Collyer, 1754AD/19.

Of the 129 men aged 20 or above in the parish in 1831, 16 were employed in retail, trade or a handicraft.[429] There were three wheelwrights' shops and two blacksmiths' shops in 1840.[430] Two decades later the parish could support three blacksmiths, four carpenters and wheelwrights, with one apprentice, two shoemakers, two tile and brick makers, and four bricklayers.[431] The Lawes brothers established the Southrope Steam Works *c.*1878, cutting their own wood, making carts and wagons, and undertaking general smithery and carpentry.[432] There was an individual making agricultural implements by 1901.[433]

A brick works was established on Herriard common *c.*1742,[434] perhaps that which gave its name to Brick Kiln Copse, near East Common. Another brick kiln was erected at Nashes Green *c.*1797, when George Purefoy Jervoise began undertaking major work on Herriard House and the surrounding grounds.[435] Neither were marked on a map of 1840, presumably having fallen into disuse before that date.[436] A brickworks, with a kiln and clay pit, had been established at East Common by 1871, but it was said to be disused by 1894.[437]

A sawmill and timberyard were established at Manor farm by 1891, apparently equipped with a steam-powered saw by 1901.[438] The site of this estate sawmill has been run by a private company since *c.*1990. In 2025, as part of AVS group, it specialised in fencing and landscaping supplies.[439] Since the late 20th century, a number of other estate buildings have been let to commercial tenants, taking advantage of the proximity of the parish to Basingstoke. The former station site was converted into a small commercial yard, in 2025 accommodating a joinery business. Other businesses based in Herriard in 2025 included a cabinet maker,[440] a cheese maker,[441] another joiner,[442] and a sofa shop.[443]

There was a shop in the village in 1865,[444] and a shop with a bakery was established

429 *Abstract Pop. Rtns, 1831,* 566–7.
430 HRO, 21M65/F7/115/1.
431 Census, 1861.
432 *Kelly's Dir. Hants.,* (1885, 1889, 1898 edns).
433 Census, 1871; 1901.
434 HRO, 44M69/E10/38.
435 HRO, 44M69/E13/3/17.
436 HRO, 21M65/F7/115/2.
437 OS Map 6", Hants. XXVII.SW (1871, 1897 edns).
438 Census, 1891, 1901; OS Map 6", Hants. XXVII.SW (1897 edn).
439 *AVS Basingstoke,* https://www.avsfencing.co.uk/avs-branch-basingstoke (accessed 4 Mar. 2025).
440 *F.B. Design,* https://www.fbdesign.co.uk (accessed 4 Mar. 2025).
441 *Hampshire Cheese Company,* https://hampshirecheesecompany.co.uk (accessed 4 Mar. 2025).
442 *Chipandell,* http://www.chipandell.co.uk (accessed 4 Mar. 2025).
443 *Sofas and Stuff,* https://sofasandstuff.com/showrooms/basingstoke-hampshire (accessed 4 Mar. 2025).
444 *Harrod's Dir. Hants.* (1865 edn).

by 1871, still trading in the middle of the 20th century.[445] The arrival of the railway encouraged the establishment of a coal merchant at the railway station.[446] A coal merchant and haulage business had been established at the New Inn by 1911,[447] and had apparently added petrol and oil sales by 1939.[448] A petrol station was erected south of the inn in the later 20th century,[449] but has since been demolished.

Businesses with a focus on environmental services and the production of sustainable energy were established at Bushywarren Lane in the early 21st century. An anaerobic digestion plant was established to convert food waste into gas and fertiliser. Next door, a composting business converts green waste into fertiliser. A solar park constructed in a neighbouring field stands in Ellisfield parish.

445 Census, 1871, 1901; *White's Dir. Hants.* (1878 edn); *Kelly's Dir. Hants.* (1898, 1927 edns); TNA, RG 101/2371H, p. 5; Owen White, unpubl. hist. of Herriard, *c.*2002.
446 *Hants. & Berks. Gaz.* 12 Oct. 1901.
447 Census, 1911.
448 HRO, 63M83/B30/23.
449 OS Map 1:2500, SU 6744 (1979 edn).

Social Character

F OR MUCH OF the Middle Ages the parish of Herriard was divided between three different lords, the tenants of whom would have had diverging experiences. Until the 15th century the Coudray family were often absent, choosing instead to reside on their Berkshire estates, and Herriard was occasionally let to farmers. Sir Thomas of Coudray granted the manor in 1315 to James of Moun, Cecile of Beauchamp and Roger of Essex for their lives for a yearly rent of £26 for the first 15 years and £100 thereafter.[450] Nicholas at Hurste had also had possession of the manor during the 14th century, quitclaiming it Sir Thomas in 1335.[451] Sir Robert Achard and his wife Agnes, the niece of Sir Thomas, were granted the manor for their lives before 1346,[452] and it remained in their hands until 1354, when Agnes granted it back to Henry of Coudray in return for an annuity of £10.[453] Southrope lay within the royal manor of Odiham, from which the tenants had apparently largely freed themselves of most of their obligations by the 15th century. Nevertheless, many tenants in Southrope still owed rents to the lords of Herriard, who held the hamlet as tenants of the Crown. The third estate, Herriard Grange, was close enough to be managed directly from the priory of Wintney, although from the early 15th century the priory's land was increasingly in the hands of tenants.[454]

Through their family connections and public offices, the lords of Herriard brought parishioners into contact with regional and national affairs. Sir Peter Coudray and his son Sir Thomas Coudray both had important military careers, which probably kept both away from Herriard for long periods.[455] Edward Coudray, who established himself through service to successive bishops of Winchester, served as sheriff and knight of the shire for Hampshire early in the 15th century. In the 16th century the manor was acquired by the Paulet family, cousins of the marquesses of Winchester, whose descendants also owned Herriard Grange. From the 16th to the 19th century,

450 HRO, 44M69/C252.
451 HRO, 44M69/C76.
452 *Feudal Aids*, II, 330.
453 HRO, 44M69/C125; 44M69/C266–7; 44M69/C762.
454 Hare, 'Nuns of Wintney', 197–8.
455 P. Jefferies, 'The Medieval Use as Family Law and Custom', *Southern History*, I (1979), 51, 53.

Paulet and his descendants the Jervoises served as sheriffs and sat in Parliament.[456] Despite this service outside Herriard, the extensive archive of the Jervoise family demonstrates the close personal interest that successive lords took in the parish.

We know little about the early residents of Herriard, although in 1086 the manor was occupied by families of villeins, bordars and a single slave.[457] Although no survey of the manor survives, early deeds record the names of tenants in Herriard and Southrope from the early 13th century onwards. One of the more substantial of these was Serlone of the Heath (*Brueria*) who had held 1½ virgates, which subsequently formed part of Herriard Grange.[458] In Southrope one virgate was held by William of Bagmore, whose son John conveyed it *c*.1220 to John, son of Geoffrey of Lagguleus.[459] Several larger tenements were granted to support younger members of the lord's family. Richard of Herriard granted a virgate *c*.1240 to his niece and nephews, and Nicholas of Sifrewast granted ½ virgate to Richard, son of John of Herriard, in the middle of the century, whilst Lewis (*Lodowic*) of Herriard held 1½ virgates and 3 a. of wood in the 1260s.[460] However, the Aymer of Herriard who had held ½ virgate in Herriard in villeinage earlier in the century was presumably not a member of the family.[461] Tenants known to have held larger estates in the middle of the century included the virgaters John of Henwood and Nicholas of the Hurst, and the half-virgater Elias the Hunter (*Vanator*) held ½ virgate.[462] Other tenants of Herriard named later in the century include Henry Cockeshulle, Ralph Tholly of Bistlesham, and William Red.[463] In Southrope a family took their name from the ½ virgate they held at a place called Aslond.[464] Later in the 13th century one virgate in Southrope was held by John of Bovile, whilst Ralph of Besevlye and John of Dogmersfield held ½ virgate each.[465]

During the Middle Ages several families acquired enough wealth and status to afford them a certain degree of comfort and prominence within the parish, often taking their names from the farms that they held. We get a glimpse of the leading families from early-14th-century taxation records, when seven individuals were assessed in 1327 for the parish of Herriard.[466] The descendants of the former lords of the manor, who took their name from the parish, remained an important presence in the manor, with John of Herriard topping the 1327 assessment at 4*s*. 11*d*., whilst

456 Above, Landownership (Manor of Herriard).
457 *Domesday*, 108; above, Introduction (Population).
458 HRO, 44M69/C292.
459 HRO, 44M69/C290.
460 HRO, 44M69/C223; 44M69/C291; 44M69/C686; 44M69/C761.
461 HRO, 44M69/C295.
462 HRO, 44M69/C1; 44M69/C237; 44M69/C286–7.
463 HRO, 44M69/C307; 44M69/C314–5.
464 HRO, 44M69/C293; 44M69/C760.
465 HRO, 44M69/C309–10; 44M69/C339.
466 There was no separate assessment for Southrope.

Lewis (*Ludowic*) of Herriard was rated at 1s. 6d.[467] Although the lord of the manor, Sir Thomas of Coudray, did not appear on the list at all, his brother Ralph was rated at 2s. 6d. for his property in the tithing, whilst Nicholas at Hurst (1s. 6d.) may have held the manor as Sir Thomas' farmer at this time.[468] The remaining three men were assessed for sums between 2s. and 2s. 6d. each. Together these seven taxpayers were amongst the leading men of the manor, whose names often occur as witnesses to the conveyances of property. The tithing's total rating of 16s. 11d. was third lowest in the hundred of Bermondspit, significantly behind the assessments of South Warnborough (79s. 10d.) and Preston Candover (62s.).[469]

The Hurst family were prominent in the parish until the late 14th century, when their property was acquired by the Coudrays.[470] The Herriard family had also been eclipsed in influence by this date, although the last piece of Herriard property remained in the family's hands until it was acquired by the Coudrays in the early 15th century.[471] The family of Lee or Lye first come to notice in the middle of the 13th century,[472] and sealed their position with marriage into the Herriard family later in the century.[473] In the late 13th century Adam of the Lee's possessions in Southrope included a fold for 100 sheep,[474] whilst Thomas at Lee served as the bailiff of Herriard Grange in the 14th century.[475] The family's absence from the list of Herriard taxpayers of 1327 can presumably be explained by their residence in Southrope. By the late 15th century the Lees were already claiming a higher degree of status than their neighbours. Peter at Lee was described as a yeoman in 1486,[476] and his son John referred to himself as a gentleman in the following decade.[477]

As many as 29 inhabitants were assessed for the subsidy of 1524, divided almost equally between the two tithings of Herriard and Southrope, although the total value of the property assessed in Herriard (£5 8s. 6d.) was three times more than in that of Southrope (£1 14s. 8d.).[478] In Herriard the lord of the manor, Peter Coudray, was assessed 5 marks (£3 6s. 8d.) for land worth a total of 100 marks (£66 13s. 4d.), whilst John Lee was assessed 35s. for £35 worth of goods, the two men together contributing more than £5 of the total amount assessed on the tithing, and more than two-thirds of the total assessed on the parish. Eleven other inhabitants were assessed for goods

467 The Lewis who held 1½ virgates in the 13th century was dead *c.*1280: HRO, 44M69/C333.

468 HRO, 44M69/C52; 44M69/C76.

469 *Hants. Tax List, 1327,* 41.

470 HRO, 44M69/C205; 44M69/C209.

471 HRO, 44M69/C436.

472 HRO, 44M69/C239; 44M69/C324.

473 HRO, 44M69/C363.

474 HRO, 44M69/C5.

475 HRO, 44M69/E1/2/48.

476 HRO, 44M69/C685.

477 HRO, 44M69/C470; 44M69/C764.

478 J. Sheail (ed. R.W. Hoyle), *The Regional Distribution of Wealth in England as Indicated in the 1524/5 Lay Subsidy Returns,* List and Index Soc., special sers, 29 (1998), pp. 119, 130.

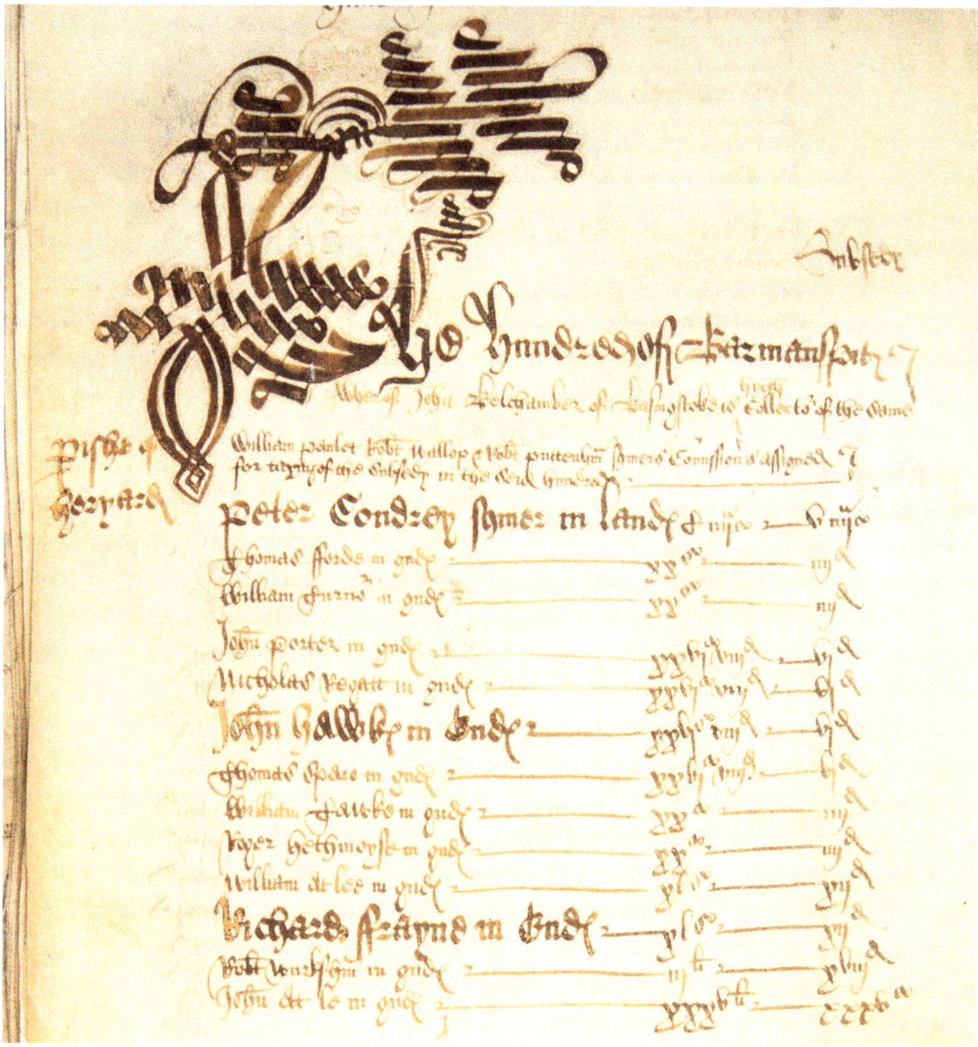

Fig. 26. Lay subsidy of 1524 for Herriard (excluding the tithing of Southrope). TNA, E 179/173/183, rot. 12d.

worth between £1 and £3.[479] In Southrope the leading resident was Peter Wise, assessed 8*s.* for goods valued at £16. John and Christian Lee were each assessed 5*s.* for land worth £5, whilst William Hyde's free land, valued at £4 13*s.* 4*d*, was assessed at 4*s.* 8*d*. Nine more residents were rated sums between 4*d*. and 1*s.* 6*d*. for goods ranging between £1 and £3 in value, and three labourers were assessed 1*s.* each for wages of £1.[480]

Sixty years later only the most substantial landowners were assessed for the subsidy.[481] Foremost amongst these were the lord of the manor, Richard Paulet,

479   TNA, E 179/173/183, rot. 12d.

480   TNA, E 179/173/183, rot. 32.

481   *Hants. Lay Subsidy, 1586*, 53.

and his mother Katherine, together assessed for land worth £12. In neighbouring Southrope Richard Lee was assessed for land worth £9, whilst his relation Stephen Lee was assessed in Herriard for £3 in land. Two other men were assessed for land held in Southrope, John Hyde at £5, and Reginald Goodier at 20s., who described himself as a yeoman.[482] A sixth man, Roger Hale or Hall, was assessed for the value of his goods (£3) rather than land. He described himself as both a carpenter and a yeoman in 1597.[483] Early in the 17th century Paulet surveyed the principal landowners and occupiers in the parish, listing 12 freeholders in the parish besides himself, with estates ranging greatly in size. The largest was the 7 yardlands of Lee farm, measuring 288 a. and held by Richard Lee, followed by the marquess of Winchester's Herriard Grange (c.250 a.), most of which was also let to Lee. Three more freeholders, Richard Yardley, John Lee, and Christopher Hyde, held farms of more than 100 a. each, whilst another five each held a yardland of approximately 30–40 a. The final two men held smallholdings of 5 a. or less.[484]

Surviving probate records from the early 16th century onwards provide further insights into the wealth and material culture of Herriard. When John Booth (*Bowyth*) died in 1509 he could leave over 60 sheep to relatives and friends,[485] whilst John Lee of Herriard bequeathed over £14 in 1524, predominantly to his son John, but also leaving £1 to a servant.[486] Detailed inventories of many inhabitant's possessions at the times of their deaths reveal that even the wealthier of the parishioners often possessed very few items of comfort or luxury. In the middle of the 16th century, the freeholder William Hyde possessed a feather bed, with a painted tester or canopy to accompany it, but his house was otherwise furnished with wooden chairs and benches.[487] Alice Lee's possessions in 1576 included ten silver spoons, a sheet of Holland cloth, and German plate armour, but also wooden stools and pewter plates for everyday use.[488] John Lee of Hurst described himself as a yeoman at the time of his death in 1615, and left possessions worth £136, but his only concession to luxury were three featherbeds.[489] The possessions of his contemporaries George Hall (d. 1620) and Lawrence Madgewick (d. 1621), both described as yeoman, did not include even this degree of comfort, despite both being wealthy.[490]

Unsurprisingly, the possessions of the occupants of the manor house set them apart from even the wealthiest of parishioners. The 1528 will of Dorothy Coudray, widow of the last Coudray lord of the manor, hints at a greater degree of comfort and

482 HRO, 44M69/E2/18.
483 HRO, 44M69/E2/12.
484 HRO, 44M69/E1/1/9.
485 HRO, Will of John Bowyth, 1509B/04.
486 HRO, Will of John Atlee, 1524B/04.
487 HRO, Will and inventory of William Hyde, 1549U/033.
488 HRO, Will and inventory of Alice Lee, 1576B/047.
489 HRO, Will and inventory of John Lee, 1615A/48.
490 HRO, Will and inventory of George Hall, 1620A/038; Will and inventory of Joan Richards of North Warnborough, 1621AD/54.

conspicuous wealth, with bequests of silver plate, a feather bed, and £20 in money to each of her three daughters.[491] A century later the dowager Lady Anne Paulet owned armour, numerous books, tapestries, painted furniture and embroidered cushions, silver plate, petticoats of silk trimmed with gold, satin gowns and velvet cloaks trimmed with fur.[492] When Sir Thomas (I) Jervoise died in 1654, there were several suites of brightly-coloured and upholstered furniture, complete with chairs, stools, couches, carpets and cushions, including one suite of exotic Turkish furniture. All of these were complemented with expensive tapestries.[493] The different experiences of the Jervoise family and their tenants is revealed in the household accounts of Lady Lucy Jervoise, which in 1618 included purchases of oysters, lobsters, currants, liquorice, and exotic spices including pepper, cinnamon, turmeric, aniseed, and ginger.[494]

The gap between the occupants of the manor house and their tenants is illustrated by the hearth tax of 1665, which emphasise the image of a parish divided into a northern half occupied by a handful of sizeable properties, and a more populous southern half occupied by numerous small cottages, with many inhabitants too poor to pay the tax, although large farmhouses could still be found here as well. Preeminent amongst his neighbours was Capt Thomas (II) Jervoise, who was charged for 25 hearths, more than all of the other hearths in the tithing of Herriard combined, and a quarter of the total of chargeable hearths in the parish. Even when ineligible hearths are included, Herriard House represented more than a fifth of the total number in the parish. Taken as a whole, there were 46 hearths charged in Herriard, divided between just six properties, and 70 hearths in Southrope (including 16 that were exempted for poverty), divided between 38 houses, revealing the weight of population in Southrope and the weight of wealth in Herriard. After the manor house, one farm was charged for 12 hearths, and another four properties, including the vicarage, were charged for six hearths each, divided equally between the two tithings. The other three properties in Herriard each had three hearths, as did three of the remaining 20 chargeable properties in Southrope. Most of the remaining chargeable properties in Southrope had just one hearth, as did all but one of the 15 cottages that were excused payment of the tax.[495]

Lee Farm was a substantial building, perhaps that assessed as having 12 hearths in 1665, and comprising a hall, a parlour, a kitchen, three upstairs chambers, a long gallery, two butteries, a brewhouse, a millhouse, a malthouse, and stables.[496] Hydes Farm, rated at six hearths, contained a hall, a parlour, a kitchen, four upstairs chambers, two butteries, and a milkhouse, with accommodation for servants, and

491 TNA, PROB 11/22/510.
492 TNA, PROB 11/131/750.
493 TNA, PROB 11/241/599.
494 HRO, 44M69/E6/85.
495 *Hearth Tax, 1665*, 208–9, 218–9.
496 HRO, Will and inventory of Henry Jarvis of Lee, 1682A/048.

a garret for wool.[497] From the later 17th century probate inventories indicate that prosperity increasingly translated into increased comfort at home. Items recorded included the carpets, curtains, upholstered chairs and a couch, a sideboard, and a mirror belonging to Henry Jervoise of Lee farm,[498] or the mirror, cushions, and clock belonging to the Nathaniel Hyde.[499] Even Richard Page, whose total goods were valued only at £15 12s. 4d., owned a feather bed with a feather bolster and a feather pillow by this date.[500] By contrast, despite the greater value of Henry Jervoise's possessions, the plate and candlesticks dressing his sideboard were made from brass, pewter and tin, not silver or gold.

Household and Servants

The extensive archive of the Jervoise family provides a glimpse within the household, which contained not only family members but also numerous servants. As well as employing local men and women on the estate at Herriard, it was usual to employ a number of itinerant servants in husbandry to tend to the crop and stock of manor, who might move on to another parish at the end a year of service. The accounts of 1597–8 show that over a 14-month period some 30 individuals were employed in agricultural tasks in Herriard, including ploughing, sowing, carting, harvesting, winnowing, and threshing. Of these, only a few were employed on most days, whilst some were only drafted in to work during peak times, such as during the harvest. The 30 individuals included not only the contracted labourers of the estate and the husbandmen of the parish, but also their wives, children, and even one man's maid.[501]

A large estate like Herriard attracted labouring men and their families to the parish to take up service as labourers, often entering into complicated reciprocal arrangements with the lords. Michael Moore agreed in 1599 to reap, bind and haul 11 a. of wheat in the following harvest in return for one year's accommodation for himself and his family in Sir Richard Paulet's house and pasture for one cow and two pigs, agreeing also to pay Paulet 10s. in rent for the year. At the same time, he agreed to undertake all thatching and hurdling for a whole year at a rate of 7d. a day, during which time his wife was to tend the pigs until another person was found to take over the work, and to prepare dinner for Paulet's servants.[502] In 1609 John Fry contracted to provide meals for himself and three other husbandmen or shepherds, Paulet providing to him weekly for each man 1 peck of wheat, rye or barley for bread, and 1 peck of barley or malt for beer, also allowing the milk of one cow per person, and providing each man with one pig from the store each year. Fry's wife was likewise to

497 HRO, Inventory of Nathaniel Hyde sen., 1675A/051.
498 HRO, Will and inventory of Henry Jarvis of Lee, 1682A/048.
499 HRO, Inventory of Nathaniel Hyde sen., 1675A/051.
500 HRO, Inventory of Richard Paige, 1682AD/064.
501 HRO, 44M69/E4/7.
502 HRO, 44M69/E4/59.

have one pig and the milk of one cow in return for tending Paulet's pigs and poultry, and 2 pecks more of corn if she boarded Paulet's 'boy', Silvester. At harvest time Paulet could require Fry to board four more labourers, who were to be provided with corn at the same rate as the other servants, and Fry was to have 18*d*. a week for each extra labourer.[503] Paulet similarly contracted with Roger King for his good service, agreeing to provide King with certain rooms in his house, together with an adequate supply of firewood and the milk of 12 cows, in return for managing Paulet's barns, keeping an account of Paulet's crops, providing fodder for the cattle, repairing breaks in the hedges, and procuring butter and cheese for Paulet's household, paying £16 in rent to Paulet.[504] A draft contract between Sir Thomas (I) Jervoise and Robert Goodwin reveals more about provisions for the household husbandmen. Goodwin was to contract for the milk of 20 cows for one whole year, at a rent of £35. He was also to provide the diet for all of Jervoise's husbandmen, receiving each week for each man 1*s*. 6*d*. in money, one peck of wheat and one peck of barley, and one peck of salt, one peck of oatmeal and 1 lb of hops each year. Goodwin was also to have one fat pig at slaughter time, and 10 lb of candles for the year.[505] Such arrangements continued in the later 17th century. In 1676 Mary Wigg rented the milk of 20 cows at £30 a year, whilst agreeing in return to feed five serving men, worth almost £20. Besides this, her son was employed within the household for the whole year, earning £4, and she provided her maid for 27 days of weeding and 13 days of harvesting on the demesne,

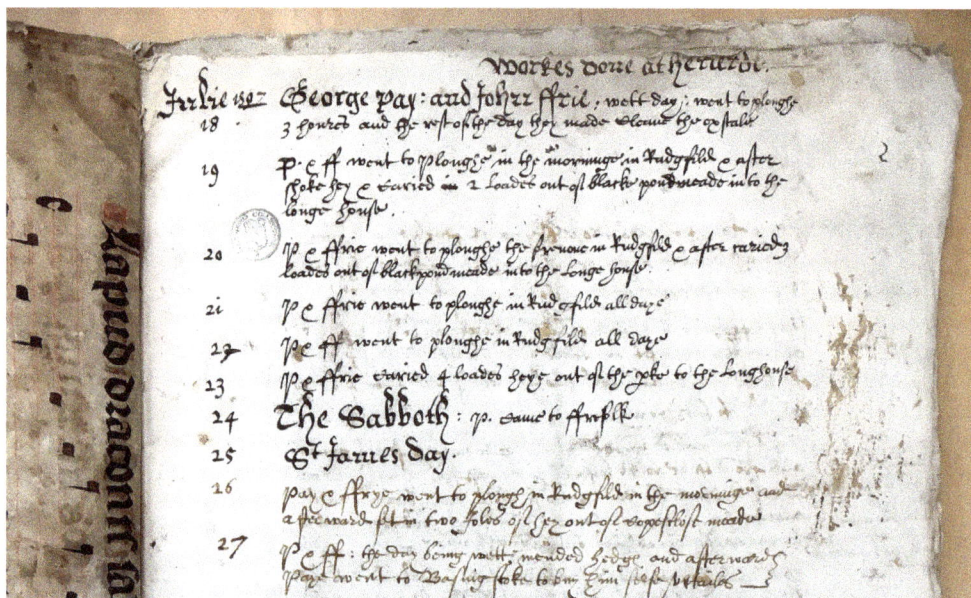

Fig. 27. Detail from a daily work notebook, 1597–8. HRO, 44M69/E4/7.

503   HRO, 44M69/E4/6.
504   HRO, 44M69/E4/68.
505   HRO, 44M69/E6/19.

at 15s.[506] Although no distinction is made in the accounts between domestic servants and farm workers, in 1678 the household employed seven women and six men as servants; 20 years later there were ten male and six female servants at Herriard.[507]

To help oversee their affairs, both in the field and in the house, the lords employed a succession of bailiffs and stewards. Sometimes the documents reveal little to us beyond the names and precision of the estate's bailiffs, men like Henry Barnard, John Porter, and John Andrews, all of whom served during the 1650s.[508] On other occasions documents provide glimpses beyond the account books. Two examples from the 17th century, James Sambourne and Thomas Austin, demonstrate that the relationship between master and servant also entailed confidence and even intimacy. Employed by Sir Richard Paulet by 1594,[509] Sambourne was the son of a clergyman of the same name.[510] By the turn of the century he was acting as tutor to a young Thomas (I) Jervoise, and was implicated by Sir George Wriothesley when he accused Sir Richard Paulet of a nefarious plot to seduce Jervoise into marrying Paulet's daughter Lucy.[511] Sambourne remained in his role after the wardship of Jervoise had been transferred from Wriothesley to Paulet, whose wife Lady Anne praised him for his care of their ward; he hoped in return that he would remain with Jervoise for a long time.[512] Sambourne continued to enjoy the patronage of Paulet, serving as curate at Herriard from 1605,[513] and then being presented by Paulet to the rectory of Upper Clatford in 1609.[514] Despite his ecclesiastical preferments, Sambourne combined his clerical duties with continued service as steward and receiver to first Paulet and then his former pupil Thomas Jervoise for the next two decades, until his death in 1626.[515]

No-one epitomised the complexity of the relationship between master and servant more than Thomas Austin, steward of the estate during the late 17th and early 18th centuries. His father, another Thomas Austin originally from the Jervoise manor of Northfield (Worcs.), had served as bailiff and steward to Capt Thomas (II) Jervoise in the years after the Restoration, producing detailed annual accounts for the family estates in Hampshire, Wiltshire, and Worcestershire.[516] The elder Austin had apparently returned to Northfield by 1681, where he died in 1688.[517] It is not

---

506 HRO, 44M69/E7/145.
507 HRO, 44M69/E7/144.
508 HRO, 44M69/E6/8/1–23; 44M69/E7/2.
509 HRO, 44M69/E4/127.
510 HRO, 1603B/51.
511 HRO, 44M69/F4/18/4.
512 HRO, 44M69/F2/9/9.
513 HRO, 44M69/J9/6
514 In the meantime, he was instituted briefly to the rectory of Gratley: *CCED*, no. 75,412; Location no. 14,803.
515 HRO, 44M69/E6/7, 69–74; 44M69/F4/18/19; Inventory of James Samborne of Upper Clatford, 1626AD/144.
516 HRO, 44M69/E7/3, 31; *VCH Worcs.* III, 195–6.
517 HRO, 44M69/F5/4/1; Library of Birmingham, EP 14/2/1/2.

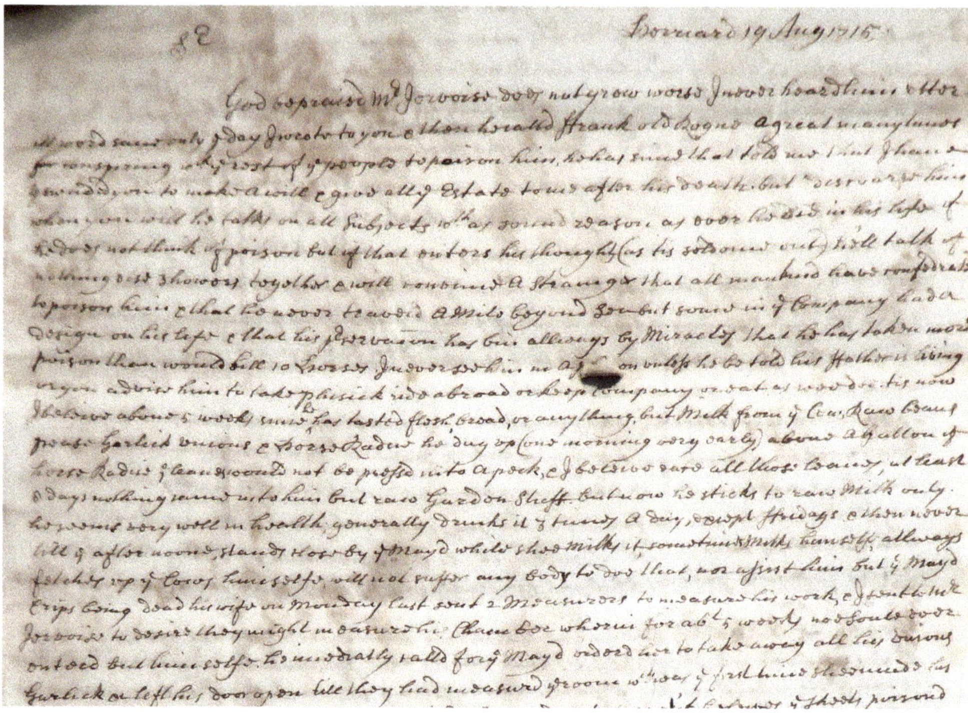

Fig. 28. Detail from a letter from Thomas Austin to Thomas (III) Jervoise, referring to Tom (IV)'s fear of poisoning, and his new eccentric diet, 1715. HRO, 44M69/F6/2/1/2/22.

clear when the younger Austin stepped into the role, but it was probably in the late 1670s, when he was still in his early 30s. For the next 40 years, until Austin's death in 1717, he played a pivotal role in the Jervoise household for both Capt Jervoise and then for his son Thomas (III). The extensive correspondence particularly of the latter preserved in the family archive at Herriard reveals the sensitive nature of the relationship between master and servant.

Many of their letters deal with important matters concerning the Jervoise estate around the country, but particularly at Herriard, Britford (Wilts.), and Northfield. In the later years of Capt Jervoise's life, Austin appears to have served as his amanuensis, transcribing the old man's concerns not only about estate matters but also about his children's extravagant lifestyles and their proposed marriages.[518] When the lord was away from home, it was the steward who would relate to him news of his family, as well as updating him with developments in the county, especially concerning local elections.[519] This was particularly true during the long absence of Thomas (III) in the Netherlands and Germany for several years, beginning in 1711.[520] The letters of Jervoise in return to his servants were also not restricted to matters of business, as the absent squire poured out his frustrations over the elopement of his daughter, and

518   HRO, 44M69/F6/1/1.
519   HRO, 44M69/F6/2/1–23.
520   HRO, 44M69/F6/2/12.

made delicate arrangements to manage his eldest son's increasingly erratic behaviour. Despite the unequal nature of their relationship, Jervoise's letters make clear that he was reliant upon the good service and care of Austin in the face of his other troubles, describing him as 'the only person I have to confide in for the management of my affairs'.[521] The position was increasingly stressful for Austin, who was not only his servant but also his creditor, having mortgaged Jervoise's estates in 1710 for £8,000, whilst simultaneously he found himself placed squarely between Jervoise's other angry creditors and his absent master.[522] It was even said in 1713 that Daniel O'Carroll, the violent husband of Jervoise's estranged daughter Betty, travelled to Herriard to kill him.[523] Austin's later letters to Jervoise reveal his angst that his service to Thomas might risk impoverishing his own family,[524] and when he died his son Samuel was forced to endure a long battle with Jervoise for settlement of his debts.[525]

Since 1800

Of the 75 individuals for whom some occupation is noted in Herriard by the 1801 census, 58 were chiefly employed in agriculture and 17 were chiefly employed in trade or handicrafts, but it records nothing about the remaining 255 occupants.[526] The 1831 census aimed to provide more information. It emphasises the continuing importance of agriculture in the economy of the parish, providing employment for 55 of 76 resident families. Of the 129 men aged 20 or over, 87 were occupied as agricultural labourers, employed by seven farmers. Another 16 men worked in trade or handicrafts, there were five male servants, and two educated men (presumably including the incumbent or his curate). Domestic service also provided employment within the parish for 13 women or girls, and one male under the age of 20.[527]

In the middle of the century, more than two-thirds of the workforce continued to be employed in agriculture, with four farmers employing 62 agricultural labourers, whilst another eight men and boys were employed as general labourers, including on the roads. The 1851 census reveals the continuing survival even at this date of service in husbandry, where unmarried farm workers lived in the farmhouse.[528] Seven farm servants lived at Manor farm, three at Lee farm, and six were accommodated in a servants' cottage at Grange farm. The wealth and status of the lord of the

521 HRO, 44M69/F6/2/12–15.
522 HRO, 44M69/D1/6/A33.
523 HRO, 44M69/F6/1/20.
524 HRO, 44M69/F6/2/1/2/31.
525 HRO, 44M69/F6/11/19; 44M69/F6/11/36.
526 *Abstract Pop. Rtns, 1801*, 319.
527 *Abstract Pop. Rtns, 1831*, 566–7.
528 A. Kussmaul, *Servants in Husbandry in Early Modern England* (Cambridge, 1981); A. Howkins and N. Verdon, 'Adaptable and sustainable? Male farm service and agricultural labour in Midland and Southern England, *c.*1850–1925', *Econ. Hist. Rev.* 61 (2008), 467–95.

manor and of his tenant-famers provided many opportunities for employment in domestic service, especially for women and girls. Herriard House employed 18 domestic servants, all resident under the roof, of whom 12 were women, including a housekeeper, two nurses, a cook, and eight maids, whilst six men were employed as a butler, a coachman, two footmen, and two grooms. The other large farms in the parish provided opportunities for the employment of women in domestic service, with a total of nine employed at Manor farm (3), Grange farm (3), including a governess, East farm (1), Lee farm (1), and at the home of the curate (1). Only one man, a carpenter, was employed in craftwork, whilst there were two elderly women living upon independent means.

Agriculture and other work on the estate continued to provide employment for most employed residents at the start of the 20th century. Mr Jervoise and seven farmers occupied 63 men in a variety of agricultural roles, whilst the estate also employed bricklayers, carpenters, sawyers, a thatcher, a foreman, and a bailiff. The arrival of new technology in Herriard was marked by the employment of two men to operate the estate's steam engine. Thirteen more men worked as labourers, including two on the railway. Domestic service continued to provide numerous opportunities within the parish and was the principal occupation for women. Besides the 17 women employed as servants in the homes of wealthier parishioners, two worked at the family grocery, two as charwomen, one as a teacher, and one as a midwife. The transient character of the population was reflected in the fact that slightly less than one-third of the parishioners were born in Herriard, although numerous others had moved from nearby parishes. Nevertheless, more than a quarter of the residents were born in other counties, including individuals from as far as Lancashire and Flintshire. Nevertheless, after Hampshire the next most common county of birth was Wiltshire, from where 25 residents (7 per cent) had originated, including four from the Jervoise manor of Britford.

Herriard's location on long-distance communication routes brought travellers through the parish, occasionally causing consternation for residents. Two travellers, described as gypsies, were each fined the punishing amount of £2 in 1883 for the seriousness of the damage their fires caused to hedges in the parish when they camped on the highway in Herriard.[529] A camp of huts was set up in the parish late in the 19th century to accommodate navvies working on the new railway, leading to complaints of crime and disorder.[530] On the night of the 1901 census 16 travelling gypsies were sleeping under canvas on Bagmore Lane.[531] Two years later, a policeman encountered a group of women and children encamped by the side of the road, returning to Bristol from hop picking. They cooked their dinner over an open fire and hung their washing from the park rails, before spending the night in their vehicles, for which one member of the party was sentenced to pay a fine of 5s. or to do seven days'

529 *Reading Mercury*, 27 Jan. 1883.
530 *Hants. & Berks. Gaz.* 15 Apr. 1899.
531 Census, 1901.

hard labour.[532]

The 2001 census can provide a remarkably full statistical profile of the residents of Herriard at the beginning of a new millennium. More than half of the parishioners were aged between 30 and 64, with 22 per cent aged 17 or under, and another 16 per cent aged 65 or older. Five per cent of residents were born outside the United Kingdom or other EU nations, and 1per cent were of mixed black and white ethnicity. As with other rural communities, agriculture ceased to dominate the local economy as the 20th century progressed, and by 2001 only 12 per cent of parishioners in employment worked in agriculture or forestry. The largest sector at the start of the 21st century was real estate and business, employing almost a quarter of all workers, whilst another 11 per cent were employed in manufacturing. Some 27 per cent of workers travelled between 5km. and 10km. for work, reflecting the village's transition into a dormitory for Basingstoke, whilst only 11 per cent travelled at least 40km., despite the proximity of the parish to the M3 motorway.[533]

Communal Life

DURING THE 19TH and 20th centuries there were numerous diversions provided within the village to entertain parishioners and encourage communal life. The school room was frequently a venue for concerts, readings, and lectures.[534] Societies were founded, including a branch of the Church of England Temperance Society, and a Herriard and District Ploughman's Association,[535] whilst friendly societies held annual fetes and dinners.[536] A Herriard and Lasham branch of the Royal British Legion was established in 1931, initially meeting at the school until the opening of a hall in Southrope in 1933. As well as hosting numerous entertainments and social events for the British Legion, the hall also became the usual venue for other groups within the parish, including the local branch of the Women's Institute. A Legion Club, latterly the Herriard Ex-Services Club, was established in 1981.[537]

Friendly Societies

There were no friendly societies in the parish in the early 19th century.[538] A branch of the Hampshire Friendly Society was established at Herriard in 1851, when 45

---

532 *Hants. Observer & Basingstoke News*, 7 Nov. 1903.

533 Census, 2001.

534 *Hants. Chron.* 29 Jan. 1870; 24 May 1884; 6 Feb. 1886; 12 Feb. 1887; *Hants. Observer & Basingstoke News*, 9 Nov. 1907.

535 *Hants. Chron.* 5 Apr. 1884; 7 Nov. 1885.

536 *Reading Mercury*, 27 June 1857; *Hants. Observer & Basingstoke News*, 20 July 1907.

537 Owen White, unpubl. hist. of Herriard, *c*.2002.

538 *Poor Law Abstract, 1818*, 402–3.

Fig. 29. Fur & Feathers. © Alex Craven.

parishioners were admitted as benefit members, and all of the gentlemen and farmers of the parish joined as honorary members.[539] By 1883 there were 60 members,[540] and by 1907 there were 78 members.[541] A branch of the Ancient Order of Foresters was founded in the parish in 1878.[542] In 1907 there were 103 adult and 21 junior members.[543]

Inns and alehouses

There appears not to have been an inn at Herriard before the middle of the 19th century, when the New Inn moved from Lasham to its present location in Southrope. A licence was first issued for the Herriard premises in 1856.[544] The pub, renamed the Fur and Feathers, found business struggling in 2022 following the Covid-19 pandemic, the closure of public transport links to Basingstoke, and rising costs, and proposals were made for its conversion into a private residence. The pub closed in 2023,[545] but reopened in the following year.[546]

---

539 *Hants. Chron.* 19 July 1851.
540 *Hants. Chron.* 10 Feb. 1883.
541 *Hants. Observer & Basingstoke News*, 20 July 1907.
542 *Hants. Ad.* 20 July 1878; *Hants. Independent*, 12 Oct. 1878.
543 *Hants. Observer & Basingstoke News*, 20 July 1907.
544 HRO, 10M57/O2/22.
545 *Basingstoke Gaz.* 9 Oct. 2022; 11 Jan. 2023.
546 *The Fur and Feathers*, https://www.thefurandfeathers.co.uk/about-us (accessed 4 Mar. 2025).

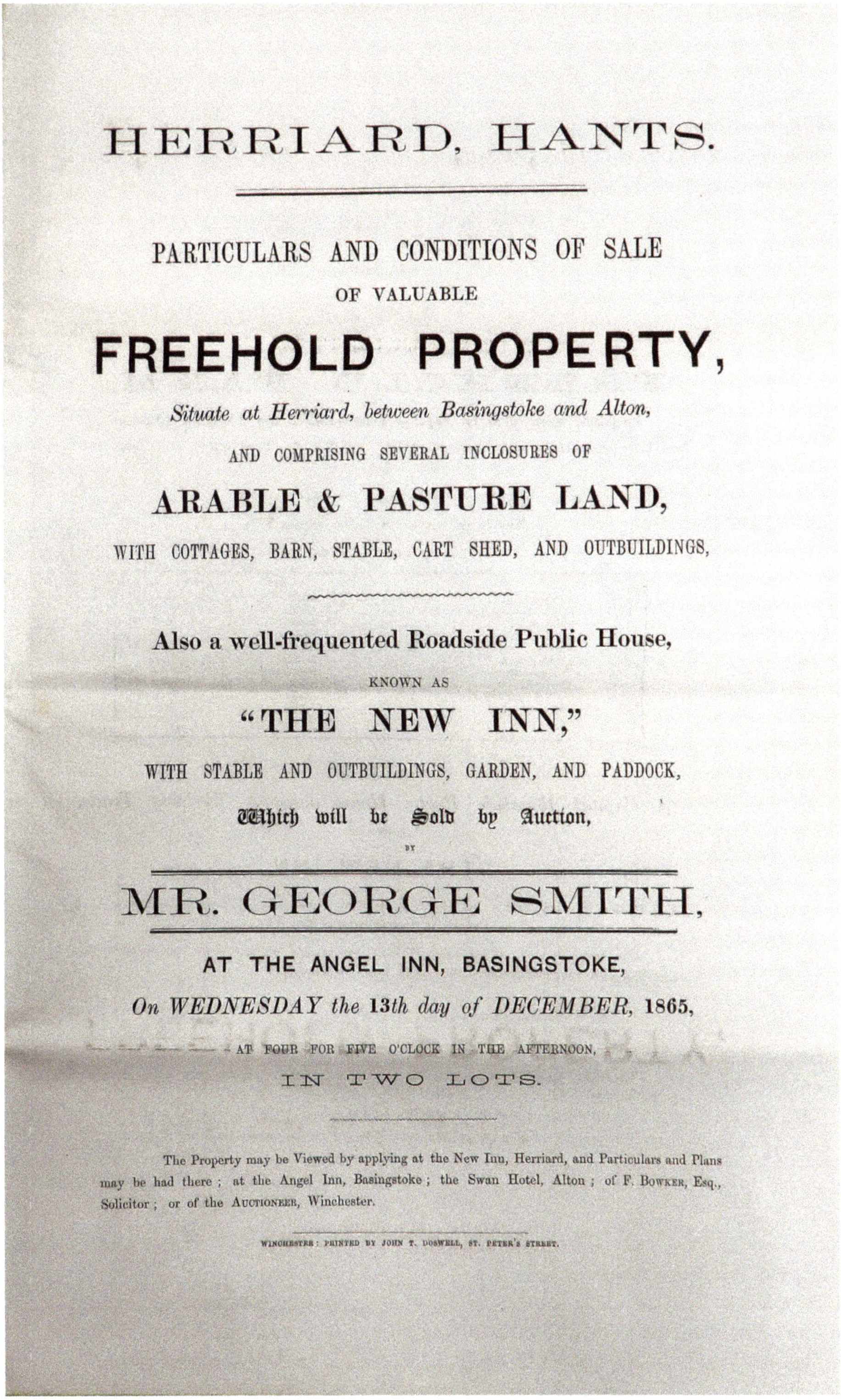

HERRIARD, HANTS.

PARTICULARS AND CONDITIONS OF SALE
OF VALUABLE

FREEHOLD PROPERTY,

Situate at Herriard, between Basingstoke and Alton,

AND COMPRISING SEVERAL INCLOSURES OF

ARABLE & PASTURE LAND,

WITH COTTAGES, BARN, STABLE, CART SHED, AND OUTBUILDINGS,

Also a well-frequented Roadside Public House,

KNOWN AS

"THE NEW INN,"

WITH STABLE AND OUTBUILDINGS, GARDEN, AND PADDOCK,

𝕎𝕙𝕚𝕔𝕙 𝕨𝕚𝕝𝕝 𝕓𝕖 𝕊𝕠𝕝𝕕 𝕓𝕪 𝔸𝕦𝕔𝕥𝕚𝕠𝕟,

BY

MR. GEORGE SMITH,

AT THE ANGEL INN, BASINGSTOKE,

On WEDNESDAY the 13th day of DECEMBER, 1865,

AT FOUR FOR FIVE O'CLOCK IN THE AFTERNOON,

IN TWO LOTS.

The Property may be Viewed by applying at the New Inn, Herriard, and Particulars and Plans may be had there ; at the Angel Inn, Basingstoke ; the Swan Hotel, Alton ; of F. BOWKER, Esq., Solicitor ; or of the AUCTIONEER, Winchester.

WINCHESTER : PRINTED BY JOHN T. DOSWELL, ST. PETER'S STREET.

Fig. 30. Sales particular for the New Inn, 1865. HRO, 10M57/SP425.

Village hall

The ancient smithy at Coopers Corner, latterly a woodstore, was refurbished *c*.1933 to serve as a hall for the newly established branch of the Royal British Legion.[547] Plans for the erection of a new hall on the site of the former railway station were rejected in 1961, and the hall has been upgraded and extended on a number of occasions since that date.[548] The building became the Herriard Village Hub in 2022.[549]

Fig. 31. Village Hub. © Barbara Large.

Sport and leisure

Herriard lay within the territory of the Hampshire Hunt, which used Herriard Common as one of its meeting places.[550] Francis M.E. Jervoise was one of three men asked to manage the affairs of the hunt in 1888 after the resignation of the master,[551] serving as joint master until 1895.[552] A horse show and gymkhana was started at Herriard Park shortly before the Second World War, and subsequently revived after the war until 1961,[553] when sponsorship for the event was withdrawn by the local

547 OS Map 1:2500, Hants. XXVII.5 (1871 edn); 1:2500, SU6745 (1978 edn); Owen White, unpubl. hist. of Herriard, *c*.2002.
548 Herriard Ex-Services Club, https://herriardexservicesclub.co.uk (accessed 4 Mar. 2025).
549 Herriard Village Hub, https://herriardvillagehub.co.uk/ (accessed 4 Mar. 2025).
550 *The Sun*, 26 Jan. 1818; *Hants. Ad.* 1 Nov. 1851; *Hants. Telegraph*, 8 Mar. 1940.
551 *Hants. Ad.* 11 Apr. 1888.
552 *Hants. Chron.* 24 Jan. 1903.
553 *West Sussex Gaz.* 23 June 1945; 8 July 1948; 14 July 1955; 5 July 1956.

branch of the Royal British Legion.[554] Motocross events were staged at Herriard in the later 20th century,[555] whilst the steep roads of the parish were also attractive to cycling clubs.[556] The peloton of the Tour de France passed through the village in 1994, travelling along the Basingstoke road en route to Portsmouth.[557]

The earliest record of organised cricket in the village comes in the middle of the 19th century. A team of men from Herriard and Ellisfield combined in 1857 to take on the Bentworth cricket club,[558] and a Herriard XI beat a team representing Lasham later in the same year.[559] Teams representing Herriard House and Herriard Grange played matches against each other in 1859.[560] There was a village cricket club by the 1880s,[561] with subscribing members by the end of that decade,[562] and by the early 20th century the team were competing in the Kempshott & District League.[563] Matches were played on a meadow to the south of the timber yard at Manor Farm, which was also used for football. The club apparently ceased to compete on a regular basis for much of the 1920s and 1930s, until it was re-founded in 1939, although it again fell into abeyance during the Second World War.[564]

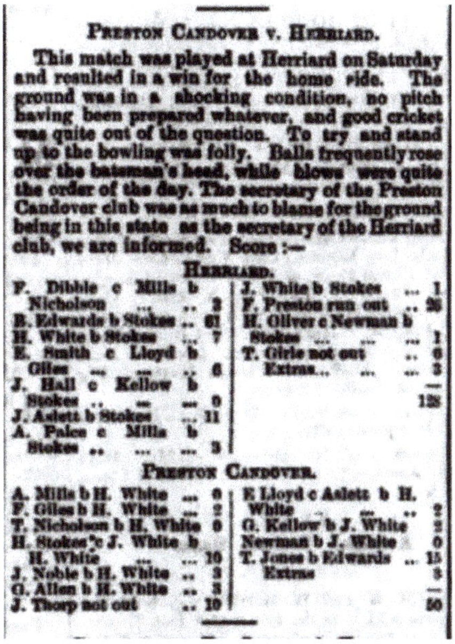

PRESTON CANDOVER v. HERRIARD.

This match was played at Herriard on Saturday and resulted in a win for the home side. The ground was in a shocking condition, no pitch having been prepared whatever, and good cricket was quite out of the question. To try and stand up to the bowling was folly. Balls frequently rose over the batsman's head, while blows were quite the order of the day. The secretary of the Preston Candover club was as much to blame for the ground being in this state as the secretary of the Herriard club, we are informed. Score :—

HERRIARD.

F. Dibble c Mills b Nicholson 3
B. Edwards b Stokes .. 61
H. White b Stokes ... 7
E. Smith c Lloyd b Giles 6
J. Hall c Kellow b Stokes 0
J. Aslett b Stokes ... 11
A. Paice c Mills b Stokes 3
J. White b Stokes ... 1
F. Preston run out .. 26
H. Oliver c Newman b Stokes 1
T. Girle not out .. 6
Extras... 3
128

PRESTON CANDOVER.

A. Mills b H. White ... 0
F. Giles b H. White ... 2
T. Nicholson b H. White 0
H. Stokes c J. White b H. White 10
J. Noble b H. White .. 3
G. Allen b H. White .. 3
J. Thorp not out .. 10
E. Lloyd c Aslett b H. White 2
G. Kellow b J. White 2
Newman b J. White 0
T. Jones b Edwards .. 15
Extras 3
50

Fig. 32. Cricket report, Hants. & Berks. Gaz., 5 Aug. 1899, p. 3. © British Library/ British Newspaper Archive. [p. 61]

A rifle club was formed in 1906, and a range was constructed at Bagmore Lane in 1907,[565] the same year in which an air club was also founded.[566] There was also a football club active in the parish by the early 20th century,[567] but it also apparently ceased to function for a time. The club was re-founded in 1940, joining the

554 Owen White, unpubl. hist. of Herriard, *c*.2002.
555 *Aldershot News*, 18 Aug. 1961; 5 Mar. 1982; *Reading Evening Post*, 26 Feb. 1986.
556 *Aldershot News*, 10 Apr. 1981.
557 *Surrey-Hants. Star*, 9 June 1994.
558 *Hants. Chron.* 11 July 1857; 29 Sep. 1857.
559 *Hants. Chron.* 19 Sep. 1857.
560 *Berks. Chron.* 3 Sep. 1859.
561 *Andover Chron.* 7 July 1882; *Hants. Chron.* 16 June 1883.
562 Owen White, unpubl. hist. of Herriard, *c*.2002.
563 *Hants. Observer & Basingstoke News*, 25 Apr. 1903.
564 Owen White, unpubl. hist. of Herriard, *c*.2002.
565 *Hants. Observer & Basingstoke News*, 5 Oct. 1907.
566 *Hants. & Berks. Gaz.* 26 Oct. 1907.
567 *Hents. & Berks. Gaz.* 19 Oct. 1907.

Fig. 33 Programme for the 10th annual Herriard Horse Show and Gymkhana, 1954. HRO, TOP159/3/4

Basingstoke & District Football League the following year, but subsequently discontinued until after the war. Following the end of hostilities, cricket matches were resumed in 1947, and football was resumed in the year after, when the football and cricket teams were merged to form the Herriard Sports Club, with matches to be played on a new sports ground behind the parish school, where a pavilion was erected in 1951. The football club competed at first in the Alton & District Football League, but moved back to the Basingstoke league early in the 1950s, and continues to compete in the district in 2025. A new pavilion was built at the sports ground in 1976, which continued in use until 2010, when the clubs moved to a new sports ground at Nashes Green.[568] Children's play facilities and a circular walk were also established at the green, making it the focus for the village's leisure and sport.[569] The facilities are maintained by the trustees of the Herriard Village Charity.[570]

Education

FROM AT LEAST the late 18th century the Jervoise family provided an elementary school for the children of the parish mostly at their own expense. The first certain reference to a school was in 1793, when Tristram Jervoise paid 3*d.* per child each week to teach 12 poor children, at a total cost of £7 16*s.* for the year.[571] Over the next 47 years, the number of children supported financially by Jervoise varied between ten and 16, although some children might only attend for a part of the year.[572] In 1800

568 Owen White, unpubl. hist. of Herriard, *c.*2002; info. from Mr J. Jervoise, 2025.
569 'Herriard Green', Village Amenities, https://herriard-pc.gov.uk/about-herriard/village-amenities (accessed 4 Mar. 2025).
570 Char. Com. no. 1080169.
571 HRO, 44M69/J9/114.
572 HRO, 44M69/J9/114.

the nine children paid for by George Purefoy Jervoise, six boys and three girls, were aged between four and nine.[573] Twelve years later Jervoise supported six boys and six girls, aged between seven and nine, the eldest of whom had been at the school for four years.[574] During all of this time the children were taught by the same teacher, one Sarah Henness, who was employed continuously from at least 1793 until at least 1840 to teach reading, writing and sewing.[575] It is unclear therefore why a parliamentary enquiry of 1818 returned that there was no school in the parish.[576] In 1835 the school was open daily and attended by 22 pupils, of whom 13 were paid for by George Jervoise, one more by the vicar, and the remainder by their parents.[577]

During this time the school was presumably accommodated at the house north of Hydes Farm that Sarah Henness occupied with her family.[578] A new schoolroom and an adjoining teacher's house was erected in the Gothic style c.1850–1 south of Manor Farm.[579] Under new rules adopted at the same time, the parents of poor children were to pay 1d. a week for the education of each of their children, whilst other parents were to pay 3d. a week or 5s. a quarter, depending upon their circumstances. The main objects of the school were stated to be 'lessons of piety and morality, order and industry', and parents were exhorted to provide further examples of these qualities by good example at home.[580] The Jervoises continued to meet most of the cost of the school for the next two decades, but the passing of the Elementary Education Act of 1870 necessitated a change of organisation.[581] In order to pay an increased salary to a new schoolmaster, school managers were appointed and subscriptions were raised from amongst the parishioners.[582] By 1874 the school had been set on a more 'efficient' footing, according to the terms of the act, with accommodation provided for up to 99 children and the purchase of new apparatus. Sufficient contributions towards the upkeep of the school had been raised from the parish that there had been no need to apply for a government grant. Francis M.E. Jervoise hoped that the school might thereby evade the requirement to employ a certified teacher, which he thought would be of little advantage to the children of labouring parents, and who he suggested would be driven crazy 'to have to teach such obtuse intellects'.[583] Officials at the Education Department were constrained to point out that the very purpose of the 1870 Act was to provide a better standard of education to the children of the

573 HRO, 44M69/J9/117.
574 HRO, 44M69/J9/118.
575 HRO, 44M69/E113/12/95; 44M69/E113/12/102; 44M69/E113/12/111–2; 44M69/E113/12/118; 44M69/J9/114; 44M69/J9/117–20.
576 *Educ. Of Poor Digest,* 828.
577 *Educ. Enquiry Abstract,* 846.
578 HRO, 21M65/F7/115.
579 HRO, 44M69/J9/121; TNA, HO 107/1681, f. 546v.
580 TNA, ED 21/6436.
581 33 & 34 Vic. c. 75.
582 TNA, ED 21/6436; HRO, 86M82/PV1, 21 Aug. 1871.
583 TNA, ED 21/6436.

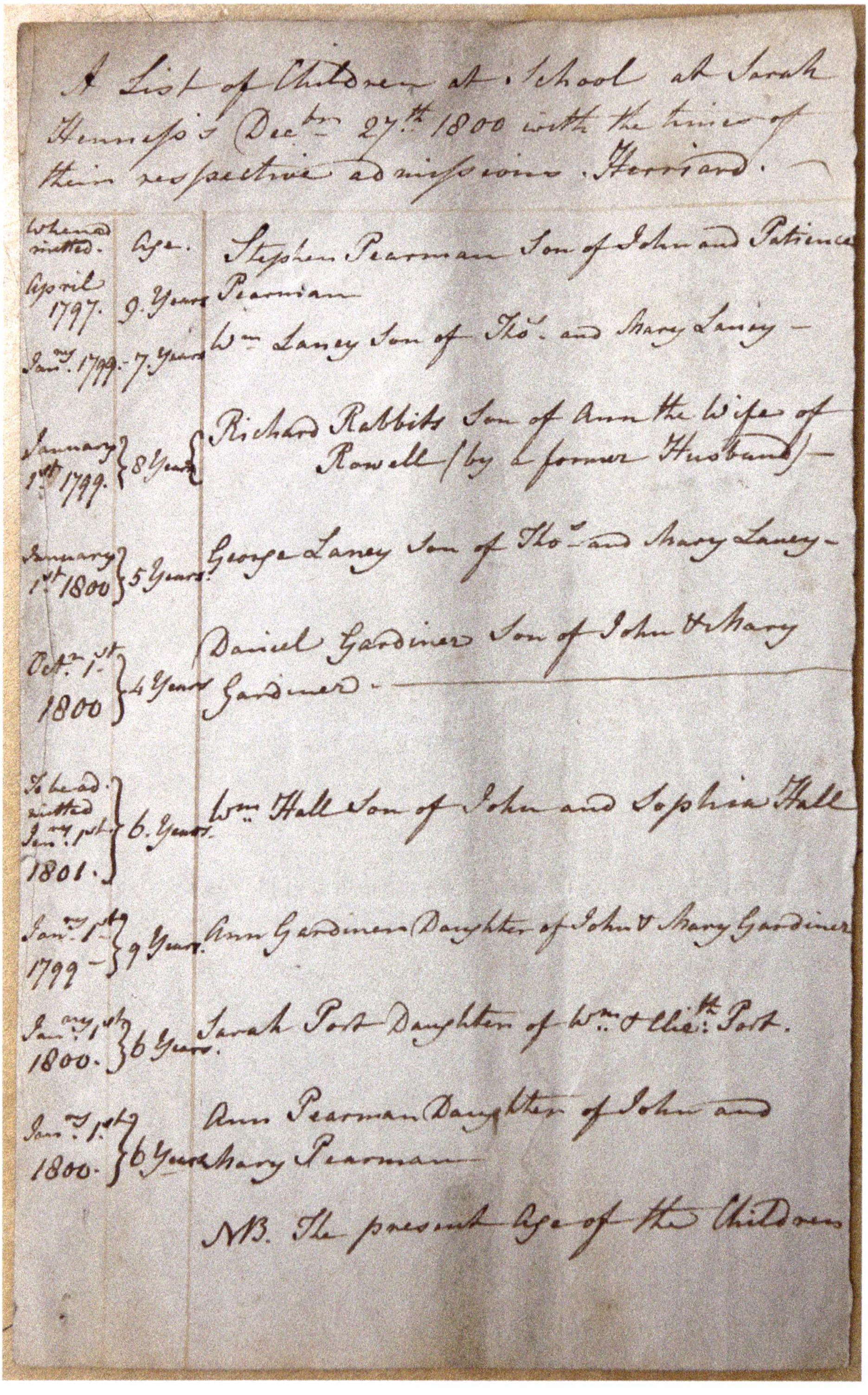

A List of Children at School at Sarah Hennesss's Decbr. 27th 1800 with the time of their respective admissions. Herriard.

When admitted	Age	
April 1797	9 Years	Stephen Pearman Son of John and Patience Pearman
Janry. 1799	7 Years	Wm. Laney Son of Thos. and Mary Laney —
January 1st 1799	8 Years	Richard Rabbits Son of Ann the Wife of Rowell (by a former Husband) —
January 1st 1800	5 Years	George Laney Son of Thos. and Mary Laney —
Octr. 1st 1800	4 Years	Daniel Gardiner Son of John & Mary Gardiner —
To be admitted Janry. 1st 1801	6 Years	Wm. Hall Son of John and Sophia Hall
Janry. 1st 1799	9 Years	Ann Gardiner Daughter of John & Mary Gardiner
Janry. 1st 1800	6 Years	Sarah Port Daughter of Wm. & Elizth. Port.
Janry. 1st 1800	6 Years	Ann Pearman Daughter of John and Mary Pearman

NB. The present Age of the Children

Fig. 34. List of children at Herriard school, 1800. HRO, 44M69/J9/117.

labouring classes. Following a positive inspection it was agreed to certify the master at Herriard, in respect of his long experience.[584]

A new headmaster was appointed in 1881, and he was soon complaining about the cramped conditions, especially in the infants' room, where overcrowding combined with summer heat caused many children to suffer from headaches. In the Autumn of 1881 the front room of the teacher's house was used as an additional classroom, although the room was too dark for some work.[585] A decision was made that year to approach the government for a grant, and the school was awarded a sum of just under £18 in 1881–2, when the average attendance was 57.[586] The value of the grant rose to almost £40 the following year,[587] falling back to £35 the year after.[588] In the following decade the government grant peaked at £56 10s. in 1891–2,[589] falling back to £48 a year later, and decreasing to less than £41 in 1897–8.[590] During that period, the average attendance was very stable, varying little from 57 in 1881–2 to 54 in 1897–8. The headmaster complained that all three teachers were forced to teach in the one large schoolroom in February 1889, for the second winter in a row, because of the lack of fire in the infants' room, to the detriment of the children's education.[591] The infants' room was enlarged in 1897, when new cloakrooms, a lobby, and a bell turret were also added.[592] Following the passage of the 1902 Education Act,[593] the school buildings were inspected by the county surveyor, who found them adequate, although noting the need for improved ventilation and clean water. The school was divided into two, a school room and an infants' room, together providing enough space for 76 children.[594]

Attendance at the school varied considerably during the early years of the 20th century, averaging 63 in 1900, rising gradually to 82 in 1908 before falling again to 58 in 1920.[595] The adoption of new pay scales by the county council in 1903 resulted in the doubling of the assistant teacher's salary, from £27 to £55 a year. The headmaster's salary, at £93, was already at a rate set by the new scales.[596] An attempt to establish an evening school in 1906 failed due to a lack of attendance.[597] The managers gave notice in 1907 to parents from Weston Patrick and Tunworth that their children would

584 TNA, ED 21/6436.
585 HRO, 44M69/J9/122, pp. 4, 6.
586 *Rep. Com. Council on Educ. 1882–3*, 661.
587 *Rep. Com. Council on Educ. 1883–4*, 641.
588 *Rep. Com. Council on Educ. 1884–5*, 557.
589 *Rep. Com. Council on Educ. 1891–2*, 633.
590 *Rep. Com. Council on Educ. 1884–5*, 88.
591 HRO, 44M69/J9/122, p. 180.
592 HRO, 86M82/PJ5–5v; TNA, ED 21/6436.
593 2 Edw. VII, c. 42.
594 TNA, ED 21/6436; HRO, 48M71/16.
595 TNA, ED 21/6555.
596 HRO, 86M82/PJ1, pp. 1–2.
597 HRO, 86M82/PJ1, p. 5.

no longer be able to attend the school,[598] perhaps in anticipation of new regulations introduced in 1908 which reduced the maximum accommodation of the school from 92 to 75.[599] The cramped conditions in the schoolroom were a cause for concern in 1914, disadvantaging the older children's learning and leaving no space for cupboards or a desk for the teacher.[600] Evening classes were commenced again three nights a week in 1919 with classes in carpentry and handicraft, although classes in arithmetic, history and geography were abandoned due to a lack of interest.[601] In 1921 H.M. Inspector reported on the good behaviour and generally good progress of the children of the school, whilst expressing concern about weaknesses in numerous areas. Two years later there had been significant improvement, although there were still concerns about the standard of arithmetic and reading.[602] The school mistress retired in 1927 after 24 years' service, followed the next year by her husband, the headmaster. Declining school attendance meant that the local education authority would only sanction the appointment of a new headmistress and not a more expensive headmaster.[603] The average annual attendance during the 1930s was 47, peaking in 1935 at 55.[604] The school at Lasham was closed c.1943, after which the children attended school at Herriard.[605]

Fig. 35. Herriard school. © Barbara Large.

598 HRO, 86M82/PJ1, p. 6.
599 TNA, ED 21/6555.
600 TNA, ED 21/6436.
601 HRO, 86M82/PJ1, pp. 38–9.
602 TNA, ED 21/29437.
603 HRO, 86M82/PJ1, pp. 45–7.
604 TNA, ED 21/6555.
605 Owen White, unpubl. hist. of Herriard, c.2002.

The nature of farm work meant that many families employed in agriculture were forced to move regularly in search of work, disrupting the children's education. The school's inspector observed in 1954 that many children then at the school had attended a number of schools. At that time, the number of children registered at the school was about 60, half of whom were brought there each day from one of the neighbouring villages by bus. The two classrooms were still overcrowded, with the infant and junior section only divided by a partition, whilst buckets were provided for toilets. Despite this, outdated furniture was slowly being replaced, and new apparatus was being purchased for the children, including musical instruments. After a succession of teachers, stability had been achieved with the appointment in 1950 of a headmistress and in 1952 of an assistant teacher, who worked well together, resulting in a high standard of work from the children.[606]

A new scheme for the school was adopted in 1955 which, at the instigation of Francis H.T. Jervoise, included a provision that one of the managers should be a person appointed by the owner of the Herriard estate, who could appoint himself. As the owner of the school and teacher's house, and the principal landowner, Jervoise argued that the onus of finding the money for running the school would necessarily fall upon him or his successors. The other five managers were to comprise the vicar, a member appointed by the diocesan education committee, one appointed by the parochial church council, one by the parish council, and one by the local education authority.[607] In response to the unsatisfactory accommodation at Herriard, the local education authority had originally determined to replace the old school with a new two-class school, but they subsequently agreed to adapt the existing building, extending the schoolroom and adding a kitchen.[608] The work was finished and the new rooms taken into use late in 1958.[609] Declining numbers of children led in 1982 to the closure of the school.[610] In 2025 Herriard lies within the catchment area for the primary school at Bentworth and the secondary school at Amery Hill, Alton.[611]

Social Welfare and Charities

N O ENDOWED CHARITIES for the relief of poverty were ever recorded in the parish,[612] but the official apparatus of the poor law was often supplemented by

606 TNA, ED 21/6555.

607 TNA, ED 21/6555.

608 HRO, 128M96/C2/49.

609 TNA, ED 21/6555.

610 HRO, 86M82/PJ8.

611 'School Catchment Area Finder', https://maps.hants.gov.uk/SchoolCatchmentAreaFinder/ (accessed 4 Mar. 2025).

612 *Abs. Charitable Donations, 1786* (Parl. Papers, 1816 (511), xvi), 1096–7; *Ret. Charities and Charitable Donations, 1829* (Parl. Papers, 1829 (274), xx); *General Digest of Endowed Charities Mentioned in the 14th Rep. of Char. Coms.* (Parl. Papers, 1873 (25-4), li), 18–19);

the philanthropy of lords of the manor and other wealthy parishioners. In the late 16th century Sir Richard Paulet gave meat, wheat and barley to his tenants in Herriard and other parishes. Each household had at least one piece of beef and one peck of grain, with some households being favoured with larger portions, or with the head, organs or entrails.[613] When Lady Anne Paulet died in 1618 she left money to pay 20 poor and honest women of the parish 1*s.* each on the four Sundays following her death, and requested that all of the food and other provisions of her household be given the poor of Herriard and Freefolk.[614] As her late husband's 16th-century calculations demonstrate, this could be a considerable store of food.[615]

Gifts of beef and wheat were made to the poor at Christmas, providing sustenance to around 50 households each year in the 1720s and 1730s.[616] In the 1740s there were also gifts of bundles, or bavins, of firewood for about 30 households,[617] and 20 loaves of bread were given out at Midsummer 1757.[618] George Purefoy Jervoise made an annual Christmas gift of food to the poor parishioners of Herriard, Lasham and Tunworth whilst he was lord of the manor. In 1799 he shared 774 lb of beef and 100 gallons of ale, worth in total £21, between the three parishes, including 204 residents (adults and children) of Herriard.[619] In the following year beef, potatoes, rice and other vegetables were made into soup to be distributed across the three parishes for two weeks before and two weeks after Christmas. Jervoise calculated that 33 gallons of

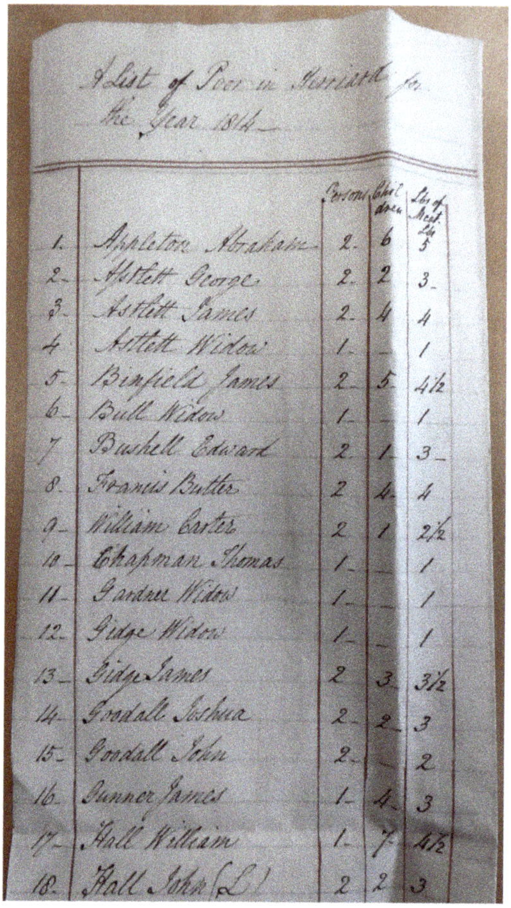
A List of Poor in Herriard for the Year 1814

		Persons	Children	Lbs of Meat
1.	Appleton Abraham	2	6	5
2.	Aslett George	2	2	3
3.	Aslett James	2	4	4
4.	Aslett Widow	1	–	1
5.	Binfield James	2	5	4½
6.	Bull Widow	1	–	1
7.	Bushell Edward	2	1	3
8.	Francis Butler	2	4	4
9.	William Carter	2	1	2½
10.	Chapman Thomas	1	–	1
11.	Gardner Widow	1	–	1
12.	Gidge Widow	1	–	1
13.	Gidge James	2	3	3½
14.	Goodall Joshua	2	2	3
15.	Goodall John	2	–	2
16.	Gunner James	1	4	3
17.	Hall William	1	7	4½
18.	Hall John (L)	2	2	3

Fig. 36. List of poor, 1814. HRO, 44M69/E13/12/106.

Digest of Endowed Charities Not in the General Digest (Parl. Papers, 1898 (131), lxvii), 26–7.

613 HRO, 44M69/E4/33.

614 TNA, PROB 11/131/750.

615 Above, Economic History (Early Modern Farming).

616 HRO, 44M69/J9/82–4; 44M69/J9/86–92.

617 HRO, 44M69/J9/93; 44M69/J9/96.

618 HRO, 44M69/J9/97.

619 HRO, 44M69/J9/104.

soup would be required each week to supply 81 adults in Herriard with two pints each and another 102 children with one pint each.[620] A survey of poor people in the parish in 1810 listed 92 adults and 121 children, including four labourers on the farm, and nine adults and ten children originally from outside the parish, who were given gifts of meat, broth and beer.[621] No part of the cow was wasted, with gifts of dripping to widows in the parish, and the sale of the hide to recoup some of the costs.[622] Besides these annual gifts, which continued at least until 1840, provision was also made at other occasions, presumably in response to economic circumstances, such as when Jervoise provided approximately 70 parishioners up to four pints of gruel each twice a week during the month of February in 1837.[623]

George Purefoy Jervoise made annual donations of clothing and blankets to the poor and needy of the parish.[624] His father, George Huddleston Jervoise Purefoy Jervoise, left £20 to the poor of Herriard in 1805,[625] of which ten guineas was spent at Christmas 1806 providing shirts, stockings, shifts and petticoats to 36 poor parishioners.[626] There were also gifts of shoes for the school children.[627] A clothing society had 84 subscribers in 1836, and 78 members in 1838, each subscribing 4s. 4d. a year, with donations also received from wealthier parishioners.[628] Accounts of the society in 1840 reveal individual subscribers were provided with various items, including hats, trousers, socks, gloves, handkerchiefs, sheets, unworked cloth, and thread, amounting to between 9s. and 14s. each.[629]

Poor Relief

The total spent on maintaining the poor in the year ending Easter 1776 amounted to c.£27, which rose to an average of c.£105 a year in the three years ending Easter 1785. Expenditure on maintaining the poor was at a similar level in the year 1802–3, when c.£104 was spent providing permanent relief to 17 adults and ten children, and occasional relief to another 12. With other costs, the total expenditure of the parish in the year ending Easter 1803 was c.£152.[630] The amount spent on maintaining the poor rose to £445 in the year 1812–3, falling to £323 two years later, when the parish

620 HRO, 44M69/E13/12/130.
621 HRO, 44M69/J9/100.
622 HRO, 44M69/E13/12/113; 44M69/E13/12/127; 44M69/J9/101; 44M69/J9/110-1.
623 HRO, 44M69/J9102.
624 HRO, 44M69/J9/105; 44M69/J9/107; 44M69/E13/12/109–10; 44M69/E13/12/114; 44M69/E13/12/116; 44M69/E13/12/129.
625 TNA, PROB 11/1436/86.
626 HRO, 44M69/J9/99.
627 HRO, 44M69/J9/115.
628 HRO, 44M69/J9/125; 44M69/E13/12/126.
629 HRO, 44M69/E13/12/127–8.
630 *Poor Law Abstract, 1804*, 450–1.

was relieving 35 people permanently and another 11 people occasionally.[631] The sum expended rose to £460 in 1824–5, and it varied little over the following four years, before rising significantly in 1829–30 to £557. It peaked two years later at £688, before falling to £506 in 1833–4.[632] National concern about the cost of poor relief in the early 1830s led to the Poor Law Amendment Act of 1834, which attempted to reduce costs by only providing relief inside a workhouse.[633] The amount expended reduced still further over the next two years, falling to £365 in 1834–5, and £241 in 1835–6.[634] Herriard was placed in Basingstoke poor law union at its creation in 1835.[635] An assistant overseer was appointed from 1840,[636] with a salary from 1886 of 5 gns a year.[637] The parish paid for 13 parishioners, seven adults and six children, to emigrate to Australia in 1852.[638]

631 *Poor Law Abstract, 1818*, 402–3.
632 *Poor Law Rtns, 1825–9*, 179; *1830–4*, 173.
633 4&5 Wil. IV c.76.
634 *Poor Law Com. 2nd Rep.* (Parl. Papers, 1836 (595), xxix (1)), App. E, 330–1.
635 *Poor Law Com. 1st Rep.* (Parl. Papers, 1835 (500), xxxv), 247.
636 HRO, 86M82/PV1, 23 Mar. 1840.
637 HRO, 86M82/PV1, 4 June 1886.
638 *Poor Law Board, 5th Annual Rep.* (Parl. Papers, 1852–3 [1625], l), 135.

Church Origins and Parochial Organization

THE CHURCH WAS probably founded early in the 13th century, when a rector was first referred to,[639] and again later in the same century.[640] Vicars were also occasionally appointed during the late 13th century, with the first reference to a vicar at Herriard in 1284,[641] whilst a deed of 1289 referred to both a vicar and a chaplain at the church.[642] A vicar was again referred to in 1310, and a successor was presented to Herriard in 1311 by the rector of the church.[643] The church was appropriated to the priory of Wintney in 1334, when a permanent vicarage was instituted.[644] The parish was subsequently always served by a vicar. The dedication to St Mary was recorded early in the 16th century.[645]

The benefice was united with Lasham in 1928.[646] The combined benefice was united in 1977 with two neighbouring benefices to create the united benefice of Upton Grey, Weston Patrick, Tunworth, Herriard and Winslade.[647] The benefice was united with several others in 2008 to form the benefice of the North Hampshire Downs.[648] In 2024 Herriard is one of four neighbouring churches within the benefice forming a distinct group, served by a dedicated cleric.[649]

Advowson and Church Endowment

Advowson

The earliest known patrons of the church were the lords of the manor, the likely founders of the church. Peter of Coudray presented his kinsman, probably a younger

639 HRO, 44M69/C226.
640 HRO, 44M69/C8; 44M69/C309; 44M69/C320.
641 *Reg. Pontissara*, 293.
642 HRO, 44M69/C10.
643 *Reg. Woodlock*, 734, 834.
644 *Cal. Pat.* 1330–4, 527; *Reg. Wykeham*, II, 553.
645 HRO, Will of John Bowyth, 1509B/04.
646 *Lon. Gaz.* 11 May 1928, 3321–3; HRO, 86M82/PB2; LPL, ECE/7/3/100694.
647 *Lon. Gaz.* 29 July 1977; HRO, 86M82/PB4.
648 *The Benefice*, http://www.northhampshirechurches.org.uk/northhampshirechurches/north_hampshire_downs_benefice-16213.aspx (accessed 4 Mar. 2025).
649 *The Benefice*, https://uptongreychurch.co.uk/the-churches/the-benefice/ (accessed 4 Mar. 2025).

Fig. 37. Interior of St Mary's church. © Barbara Large.

son, Richard, to the rectory in 1302.[650] A later lord, Sir Thomas of Coudray, granted the advowson of the parish to the priory of Wintney in 1334,[651] and convent retained

650 *Reg. Pontissara*, 150.
651 *Cal. Pat.* 1330–4, 526; HRO, 44M69/C680.

the advowson until the dissolution of the monasteries.[652] The rectory and advowson were subsequently granted in 1536 with the manor of Herriard Wintney to Sir William Paulet, later the 1st marquess of Winchester.[653] Early in the 17th century Sir Richard Paulet acquired the next presentation to a vacancy, but complained that the vicar had plotted with his successor to cause the vacancy to fall into lapse, as a consequence of which the Lord Chancellor presented in 1613.[654] The advowson descended with Herriard Grange, and was sold with the manor in 1851 by Lord Bolton to Francis J.E. Jervoise.[655] The Jervoise family were sole patrons of the united benefice of Herriard and Lasham from 1928, but have subsequently had to share patronage following later amalgamations of the benefices.[656] Since 2008 the Jervoise family have shared the advowson jointly with the bishop of Winchester, Queen's College, Oxford, St John's College, Oxford, and Mr N. McNair Scott.[657]

Church Endowment

A messuage in Herriard was held for the rent of one gillyflower and the payment of 2s. to the church.[658] The rectory was valued at £21 13s. 4d. in 1291, from which the vicar was paid £5.[659] The great tithes were valued at £2 10s. c.1341, whilst the rectorial glebe, comprising a messuage, garden and 27 a., were valued at £5 15s. 4d., and the small tithes and other dues were worth £5 15s.[660] The vicarage, including the farm of the glebe, small tithes and other dues, was valued in 1536 at £7 6s. 4d.[661] Early in the 17th century the vicar's tithes were worth £12,[662] and the vicarage was said to be worth £30 in the 1650s.[663]

The vicar's tithes were worth £28 a year in 1764.[664] The vicar was entitled to all of the tithes of the parish except those of the rectory in the early 19th century. They were valued at £153 in 1835,[665] and were commuted in 1842 for a rent-charge of £200.[666] The living was valued at £190 in 1868, £202 in 1885, and £133 in 1903. The living was valued at £300 in 1929, just before its amalgamation with Lasham, comprising £189

652 HRO, 21M69/A1/16, f. 12; 21M65/A1/21, f. 150.
653 *L&P Hen. VIII*, XI, 155.
654 HRO, 44M69/F2/14/28; below, Religious Life (Reformation to Present Day).
655 Above, Landownership (Wintney Herriard Grange).
656 *Crockford Clerical Dir.* (1977–9 edns), 349.
657 *Crockford's Clerical Dir.* (2010 edn).
658 HRO, 44M69/C331–2.
659 *Tax. Eccl.* 212.
660 *Nonarum Inquisitiones*, 122.
661 *Valor. Eccl.* II, 15.
662 HRO, 44M69/F2/14/28.
663 *Cal. Cttee for Compounding* III, 2373
664 HRO, 44M69/J9/19.
665 *Rep. Com. Eccl. Revs, 1835*, (Parl. Papers, 1835 (67), xxii), 870–1.
666 HRO, 21M65/F7/115/1.

from Queen Anne's Bounty, £107 from the ecclesiastical commissioners, and £1 in fees. The income of the united benefice was valued in 1932 at £585, and still in 1947. The value of the living was augmented in the years following the Second World War, rising to £555 in 1954, £703 in 1958, and £1,025 in 1968.[667]

Religious Life

The Middle Ages

Little is known about the religious life of the parish during the Middle Ages. The earliest known rector was a priest named Thomas, who was resident early in the 13th century.[668] Perhaps it was he who received letters from bishop Peter of Roche in 1223–4.[669] Peter of Baskerville (*Baskyvyle*) was rector of Herriard in 1256, when he was granted dispensation to hold a second benefice.[670] Baskerville, or a namesake, was still rector in 1281.[671] A vicar had been appointed by 1284 to serve the cure on behalf of the absent rector,[672] the same vicar called John who served the cure in 1289 with the assistance of a chaplain called Robert.[673] The fact that late-13th- and early-14th-century rectors sometimes appointed vicars to deputise for them suggests that the parish may have been treated as a sinecure by the incumbents. Richard of Coudray was presented to the rectory in 1302, presumably a young son of the lord of the manor, Peter of Coudray.[674] Richard was given licence to leave the parish to study in 1306, and was only finally ordained in 1309.[675] John of Sherborne was instituted vicar of Herriard in 1310.[676] Richard of Coudray resigned the rectory in 1322, when he was succeeded by Thomas of Combe, formerly the incumbent at Exton (Hants.).[677]

The rectory was granted to the priory of Wintney by Sir Thomas of Coudray in 1334, which appropriated the benefice and instituted a perpetual vicarage in the parish.[678] Coudray was also a benefactor of the church in another of his manors, granting 6 marks of rent from lands in Herriard and Ellisfield to endow a chantry in the parish church of Sherborne St John.[679] Little is known about the religious life

---

667 *Crockford's Clerical Dir.* (1868–1968 edns).
668 HRO, 44M69/C226.
669 *English Episcopal Acta IX: Winchester, 1205–1238*, ed. N. Vincent (London, 1994), 116, 118.
670 *Cal. Papal Reg.* 1198–1304, 353.
671 HRO, 44M69/C8; 44M69/C309.
672 *Reg. Pontissara*, 293.
673 HRO, 44M69/C10.
674 *Reg. Pontissara*, 150.
675 *Reg. Woodlock*, 117, 831.
676 *Reg. Woodlock*, 734.
677 *Reg. Sandale and Asserio*, 465.
678 *Cal. Pat.* 1330–4, 527; HRO, 44M69/C680.
679 *Cal. Pat.* 1334–8, 420.

of the parish during the later Middle Ages, nor do we know about the patronage of the nuns, but they may have used the benefice to support the priests attached to the convent.[680] Nicholas Brigg was vicar of Herriard early in the 15th century,[681] and John May was presented in 1494.[682] He was succeeded three years later by Richard Whenfeld.[683]

Surviving probate material of the 16th century gives us a much greater, revealing for instance the existence of altars within the church dedicated to St Michael and to St Nicholas in the early 16th century.[684] When the parishioner John Booth (*Bowyth*) died in 1509 he left 6s. 8d. to the church and another 10s. towards maintaining its fabric. He wished a black cloth embroidered with a white cross to be laid over his burial place, in front of the altar of St Nicholas, which was to be left in place for four months, together with five lights to represent the five wounds of Christ. The curate, Sir Thomas, was to celebrate a mass for his soul three times a week for three months after his death, and money was left for the Franciscans of Reading to celebrate a mass. Four sheep were also left towards the cost of maintaining a light in front of St Michael's altar.[685] The church was in the hands of the curate, Edward Frogate, c.1524.[686] Other parishioners who died in the decade before the Reformation also left money for the celebration of masses and the maintenance of lights in the parish church,[687] including Peter Coudray, the lord of the manor, who left 10 marks a year to pay a priest to sing daily masses for his soul for three years after his death. Besides his arrangements in Herriard, Coudray also left money to the four orders of friars in Winchester, and to the Franciscans in Reading.[688] His widow Dorothy similarly left money to maintain a priest to sing masses for her for three years, and also bequeathed to the church a vestment for the priest to wear when singing mass.[689] The vicar William Wynsell died c.1526, when he was succeeded by Richard Goodney.[690] Richard Gwynn (d. 1532) was the vicar in 1528 until his death.[691]

His successor Thomas Hitchcock was presented to the living in 1532, the last to be presented by the nuns of Wintney before the Dissolution.[692] By the 1540s the doctrinal upheaval of the previous decades had left parishioners unconfident when making funeral arrangements, two testators of 1545 merely directing their widows 'to

680 John Hare, 'The Nuns of Wintney Priory', 195.
681 HRO, 44M69/C428; 44M69/C442–3.
682 Reg. Langton, f. 6.
683 HRO, 21M69/A1/16, f. 12.
684 HRO, Will of John Bowyth, 1509B/04; Will of John Lee, 1523B/22.
685 HRO, Will of John Bowyth, 1509B/04.
686 HRO, Will of John Lee, 1523B/22; Will of Henry Ashton of Quarley, 1524B/04.
687 HRO, Will of John Lee, 1523B/22; Will of Henry Ashton of Quarley, 1524B/04.
688 TNA, PROB 11/22/463.
689 TNA, PROB 11/22/510.
690 HRO, 21M65/A1/21, f. 150.
691 TNA, PROB 11/22/510; HRO, Will of Richard Gwynn, 1533B/16.
692 HRO, 21M65/A1/23, f. 9.

order and dispose for the wealth of my soul as it shall be thought to her most best.'[693] William Hyde left a sheep to the high altar at Herriard in 1549, and two more towards installing seats within the church.[694] Richard Paulet showed more confidence when he made his will in the 1540s, instructing his executor to arrange for a dirge and a trental of masses to be performed on the day after his death, leaving money to pay for the priests, the bell ringers, and to procure bread for the poor. The arrangements were to be repeated one month and one year after his death, whilst more money was set aside to employ an unbeneficed priest to sing mass at the altar of the five wounds in the church every day for five years. By the time of his death *c*.1551 many of these traditional ceremonies were proscribed under the Protestant regime of Edward VI. During his life Paulet had procured books, vestments and copes in blue and red velvet, and an organ, all of which he now bequeathed to the church, leaving other vestments to churches at Weston Patrick and Winslade.[695] Throughout these tumultuous decades of the Reformation, the vicar Thomas Hitchcock was to be a constant presence, retaining the benefice until his death in 1555.[696]

From the Reformation to the Modern Day

The poverty of the living meant that the incumbents were often pluralists, holding the benefice together with one or two other local parishes. Peter Revillard, vicar in the early 1560s, is the first incumbent known to have been presented by the new patrons.[697] At around this time the parish was presented with a new silver chalice, although the identity of the donor is unknown.[698] Revillard resigned in 1564 to be succeeded by Richard Hood, also the curate at Upton Grey,[699] who was replaced two years later by a Welshman, Richard Apryce [*ap Rhys*].[700] His parishioners protested in 1567 after he had denounced them during one sermon, asserting that the congregation included 'whoremongers, backbiters and slanderers', predicting that some would hang or drown themselves for their sins within the year, and that the descendants of others would beg for their bread for four generations.[701] Apryce was deprived in 1570, when he was replaced by Bernard Blacker (vicar 1570–7), who was also incumbent at Ellisfield and Ewhurst.[702] Lewis Thomas was vicar from 1577 until

---

693 HRO, Will of John Foster, 1545B/064; Will of Peter Wise, 1545B/161.

694 HRO, Will and inventory of William Hyde, 1549U/33.

695 TNA, PROB 11/35/54.

696 TNA, PROB 11/37/316; *CCED*, no. 93,806.

697 HRO, Will and inventory of Thomas Smythe of Boldre, 1562A/54; Will of Henry Baily of Lymington, 1562B/008; *CCED*, no. 101,775.

698 P.R.P. Braithwaite, *Church Plate of Hants.* (London, 1909), 103–4.

699 HRO, 21M65/A1/26, f. 8; *CCED*, no. 107,180.

700 *CCED*, no. 105,907.

701 Christopher Haigh, *The Plain Man's Pathway to Heaven: Kinds of Christianity in Post-Reformation England, 1570–1640* (Oxford, 2007), 19–20.

702 HRO, 21M65/A1/26 ff. 79, 115; *CCED*, no. 106,089.

Fig. 38. Watercolour of St Mary's Church before restoration, c.1846. HRO, 65M89/Z120/1.

1585,[703] when he was succeeded by John Wynn. At this time, and presumably for long before, the vicar of Herriard would perambulate the parish with other parishioners at Rogationtide, stopping to read passages from the Bible at specified points on the boundaries, marked by trees or crosses erected in the landscape.[704] Wynn was later given dispensation in 1598 to hold the benefice together with the rectory of Elstead (Suss.).[705] After his departure to the south coast, Wynn farmed the living to another clergyman called Robert Bagnall.[706] It was later said, however, that he had accepted money from Sir Richard Paulet in return for allowing Paulet to appoint a curate of his choosing during Wynn's absence,[707] and it was presumably Paulet who had selected the curate, Thomas Woods, who was still at Herriard in 1607.[708] Part of the church was rebuilt in 1602, perhaps replacing the steeple which it was said had fallen down long before, when bells were also cast for the parish.[709]

Wynn's successor, Thomas Williams, was presented to Herriard in 1613 by the Lord Treasurer after the living had fallen into lapse.[710] He had married a relative of Wynn, and it was alleged by Sir Richard Paulet that the two clergymen had conspired

703 HRO, 21M65/A1/26, f. 115.
704 HRO, 44M69/F2/14/18.
705 *CCED*, no. 79,613.
706 HRO, 44M69/J9/5.
707 HRO, 44M69/F2/14/28.
708 HRO, 21M65/B1/23.
709 HRO, 44M69/J9/136; 44M69/F2/14/28.
710 HRO, 21M65/A1/29 f. 39; Andrew Thompson, *The Clergy of Winchester, England, 1615-1698* (Lampeter, 2011), 195; *CCED*, no. 96,878.

to have Williams presented to the living in succession to Wynn, despite the fact that Paulet had acquired the presentation to the next vacancy for himself. Williams was soon further in conflict with the lord of the manor when he refused to accept the previous composition rate for his tithes. Consequently, he alleged that Paulet carried out numerous vexatious actions against him, denying him certain rents previously held by the vicars, enclosing his garden with a hedge very close to his house, removing stones from the churchyard during time of worship, and using threatening and menacing language towards him and his pregnant wife. When Williams tried to appoint his own parish clerk, he was resisted by Paulet and Sir Thomas Jervoise, who objected that by removing the long-serving parish clerk he was denying an old man the little relief provided by his wages. Williams also complained that during his predecessor's time Paulet had had the vicar's seat pulled down to make room for his mother's grave, around which he erected a seat for himself that was so high that Williams said he could neither be seen nor heard during services. Meanwhile the vicar's old seat was discarded in the belfry, leaving him to find a seat wherever he could. To the objection that Paulet and his household had been attending services at Tunworth church instead of Herriard, Paulet retorted that he only went there once for the promise of a good sermon, those being 'now rare at his own parish church.'[711] Despite this, Williams remained in the living for over 30 years, although he certainly employed curates to assist him, including one John Clerk in 1622.[712] Some dissatisfaction with Williams' ministry may have lingered, however. When Sir Richard's widow, Lady Anne, died in 1618 she left money to employ four preachers to give sermons in the churches of Herriard and Freefolk on the four Sundays after her death. Amongst the personal possessions which she divided amongst her family were a collection of divine books, although only her copies of the Bible and Fox's *Book of Martyrs* were named.[713] The churchwardens acquired a new prayer book for the parish in 1624, when the communion cup was also repaired.[714]

Williams died in 1645, when James Garth was presented to the living by Parliament.[715] He was awarded an augmentation of £50 from the sequestered rectory of Herriard, but he complained in 1653 that the farmer had not paid him in over a year. Garth's augmentation was renewed in 1654 by the Commission of Triers, but he was still owed his arrears in 1655.[716] Ezekiel Lawrence, the rector of Lasham, was also acting in some capacity in Herriard during the early 1660s.[717] John Diggle was presented to the vicarage in 1664, holding it until 1683, combining it with Weston

---

711 HRO, 44M69/F2/14/28. For the dispute concerning the vicar's seat, see also HRO, 44M69/J9/20.
712 HRO, 21M65/B1/31; *CCED*, no. 106,334.
713 TNA, PROB 11/131/750.
714 HRO, 44M69/J9/22.
715 W.A. Shaw, *Hist. of the English Church During the Civil Wars and Under the Commonwealth* (London, 1900), II, 324; *CCED*, no. 7,739.
716 *Cal. Ctee for Compounding*, III, 2372–4; HRO, 44M69/J9/13.
717 HRO, Will and inventory of Robert Rivers, 1664A/080; *CCED*, no. 94,081.

Patrick from 1671.[718] Diggle recorded the presence of only a single Catholic and no Protestant nonconformists in the parish in 1676.[719] This level of conformity continued into the 18th century when Diggle's successor, Richard White (vicar 1683–1735) returned in 1725 that there were no Catholics or nonconformists in the parish.[720] More than 60 years later John Ilsley,[721] curate of Joseph Robertson (vicar 1758–1802),[722] still found no parishioners who were not conformable to the Church of England.[723] Robertson's successor in 1802 was John Orde, a cousin of the patron, lord Bolton,[724] and an absentee pluralist who was resident at his other living of Kingsclere,[725] which he exchanged in 1817 for Itchen Stoke and Abbotstone, adding Winslade in 1811, and Wensley (Yorks.) in 1829.[726] To supply the cure in his absence, Orde employed curates, including from 1810 John Hewer, rector of Tunworth and also curate at Ellisfield.[727] Hewer was still serving as curate of Herriard in 1829, when he received a salary of £70.[728]

Lovelace Bigg Wither, scion of a well-established local gentry family, was presented to the vicarage in 1830, but after he succeeded his father to the family estate at Manydown he resigned in 1835 in favour of his brother Walter.[729] The church was apparently in a poor state at this date, with the vestry considering the reconstruction of the tower in 1841, and complaining in the following year that the ceiling of the church was much decayed and would need to be entirely rebuilt, although it is not clear whether the repairs were undertaken.[730] From 1841 Bigg Wither was allowed to hold Herriard in plurality with the vicarage of Wootton St Lawrence, another ancestral parish of his family, where he was usually resident.[731] In Bigg Wither's absence the care of the parish was once more placed in the hands of a succession of curates.[732] The Elizabethan communion cup was repaired in 1850, when Francis J.E. Jervoise presented the parish with a new paten to accompany it. In the same year the parish decided to redecorate the pews and gallery within the nave, and to repair and

718 HRO, 31M48/5/1, f. 16; 21M65/A1/33, p. 101; 21M65/B1/40; 21M65/B1/43; 21M65/B1/46; 21M65/B1/48; *CCED*, no. 55,855.

719 *Compton Census*, 84.

720 *CCED*, no. 96,779; *Parson and Parish*, 70–1.

721 *CCED*, no. 78,252.

722 *CCED*, no. 95,253.

723 *Parson and Parish*, 288.

724 'Orde of Weetwood Hall', *Burke's Landed Gentry* (1894 edn), II, 1532.

725 *Doing the Duty*, 62.

726 HRO, 19M85/1; 21M65/E2/467; 44M69/D1/6M/1; *CCED*, no. 71,911.

727 *CCED*, no. 5,998; 35M48/6/1128; *Doing the Duty*, 62, 113.

728 HRO, 21M65/E6/13/80.

729 HRO, 21M65/A2/5, pp. 151–2; 44M69/D1/6M/1; *CCED*, nos 109,161 and 109,163; R.F.H Bigg Wither, *Materials for a Family History of the Wither Family* (Winchester, 1907), 57–9.

730 HRO, 86M82/PV1, 13 Apr. 1841; 22 Dec. 1842.

731 LPL, FII/182/106; FI/BB, II, f. 494.

732 HRO, 21M65/E6/13/408; 21M65/E6/13/441; 21M65/E6/13/483; 21M65/E6/13/730; 21M65/E6/13/1036; 21M65/E6/13/1185; 21M65/E6/13/1231.

paint the exterior of the tower.[733] The parish was served by the curate John Charles Morgan in 1851, when services were usually attended by 180 congregants in the morning and 137 in the afternoon.[734] Services were accompanied by music from a harmonium by 1863, when the parish chose to collect a voluntary subscription for the schoolmistress for her playing.[735] The licences of the curates all stipulated that they were to reside in the parish even though there was still no vicarage house in Herriard, although it was said that 'a good residence [was] provided by the patron' to Bigg Wither's successor, George Jones.[736]

Following their acquisition of the rectory in the middle of the 19th century, the Jervoise family were active patrons of the church, serving as churchwardens, attending

Fig. 39. St Mary's church the day before the tower was dismantled, with F. J.E. Jervoise standing in front, 1876. HRO, DC/L6/4/9.

vestry and church council meetings, expending money upon the maintenance the church, and recording its history.[737] Having first proposed the rebuilding of the decrepit church in 1873, it was thoroughly restored *c.*1876–7 by Francis J.E.

733 HRO, 86M82/PV1, 27 June 1850.
734 *Rel. Census, 1851*, 186.
735 HRO, 86M82/PV1, 6 Apr. 1863.
736 *Kelly's Dir. Hants.* (1878 edn), 284.
737 HRO, 86M82/PV1; 86M82/PP5; 44M69/J9/147; 44M69/J9/154.

Fig. 40. Drawing of St Mary's church from the south before the construction of the new aisle. HRO, 44M69/P1/78.

Jervoise.[738] Charles M. Barham was presented to the living in 1924,[739] the last vicar to be presented to the independent benefice of Herriard. During his incumbency there were three services every Sunday, including a celebration of the Eucharist at least once each week, attended by between 40 and 60 congregants, although this number rose to 100 at Easter.[740] The union of the parish with Lasham was proposed in 1926, and a subsequent inquiry found the suggestion acceptable, although the vicar was keen to recommend that the parish was unsuitable for a young – and presumably energetic – clergyman.[741] The patron, Francis H.T. Jervoise, was opposed to any unions, but the commissioners supported the proposed union with Lasham, despite his objections. The rector of the united benefice was to reside at Lasham, where there was already a parsonage, although the commissioners felt that the incumbent should reside at Herriard if a suitable house could be provided there.[742] The order took effect in 1929 following Barham's resignation.[743]

Arthur H.A. Bouchard, 7th viscount Mountmorres, was presented to the parish in 1939,[744] and he remained in the living throughout the Second World War. Due

738 Below, Church Architecture.
739 *Crockford's Clerical Dir.* (1926 edn), 73, 1842.
740 LPL, ECE/7/3/100694.
741 LPL, ECE/7/3/100694.
742 LPL, ECE/7/3/100694.
743 *Crockford's Clerical Dir.* (1933 edn), 859, 1640.
744 *Crockford's Clerical Dir.* (1939 edn), 938.

to a deterioration of his health early in 1942, Bouchard was unable to serve the cure nor to find another to serve in his place. In April of that year he apologised to the parishioners in the church magazine 'for the unavoidable dislocation of parish life due to his breakdown in health and the very great difficulty in obtaining a Locum Tenens owing to the scarcity of clergy and the many cases of illness amongst them'.[745] He recovered and in the following year he helped to oversee the establishment of a Sunday school in the parish.[746] Owen Jones, rector of Herriard with Lasham from 1954,[747] gradually introduced modest reforms into the religious life of the parish, changing the times of services to better suit the congregants, and alternating a modern liturgy with the 1662 Book of Common Prayer each week.[748] Further amalgamations took place in the late 20th and early 21st centuries. The bell tower was repaired in 2008 and the number of bells increased from three to six.[749] In the same year the parish became part of the North Hampshire Downs Benefice.[750] In 2025 the parish is grouped with three other local churches within the larger benefice, with a dedicated priest in charge, and with one service at the parish church every Sunday.[751]

Church Architecture

The oldest extant material in the church dates from the 13th century, in particular the chancel and south wall of the nave, although much of the modern structure dates from the restoration of 1876–7. The church comprises a chancel of two bays, a nave of three bays with a north aisle, and a three-stage tower at the west end, whilst a boiler house projects north from the chancel. It has tile roof walling in flint with stone dressings and stone pieces in the older walling.

Although the oldest parts of the nave appear Norman, with ashlar clasping buttresses and two small lancet windows on the south side, they are examples of a tradition that persisted late in Hampshire. The chancel is more typical of the early 13th century, whilst the late-14th-century Perpendicular east window may have been provided by Wintney priory after its acquisition of the advowson. New windows were also added in the nave. [752] Inside the church the tall chancel arch was greatly altered during the Victorian restoration, although a band of the original Early English dog-tooth pattern was retained.

---

745 HRO, 39A04/9.
746 HRO, 86M82/PP5.
747 *Crockford Clerical Dir. (1955-56)*, 633, 1519.
748 HRO, 86M82/PP5.
749 'Herriard St Mary', https://uptongreychurch.co.uk/the-churches/herriard/ (accessed 4 Mar. 2025).
750 Above, Church Origins and Parochial Organization.
751 'Parish Magazine', https://uptongreychurch.co.uk/parish-news/view-the-magazine/ (accessed 4 Mar. 2025).
752 *Pevsner North Hants.* 328.

Fig. 41. Interior of the church before restoration, 1876. HRO, DC/L6/4/10.

Fig. 42. Interior of the church after restoration, 1876. HRO, 44M69/J9/151.

Seats were installed in the church in the middle of the 16th century.[753] At the end of the century Sir Richard Paulet was said to have had the vicar's seat removed from its usual place in order to construct a large seat for himself and his family, said to have been so high that the vicar struggled to be seen or heard by the rest of the congregation. At the same time, he had the stone lifted from the vicar's grave in the chancel to cover his mother's tomb.[754] In the early 17th century it was recorded that the church's steeple had fallen down many years before and was still lying in a great heap against the side of the church, endangering the walls. The churchwardens allowed the surveyors of the highways to take the stones for the repairing of the roads in the parish, and the lord of the manor took more stones to build his dog kennels. The steeple had not been replaced in 1614, when the church had a timber tower.[755] The damage caused by the fallen steeple to the walls of the church may have been the reason why money was collected towards the repair of the west end of the church in the 1640s.[756] The tower was still a concern for the vestry in 1841, but it may have remained unrepaired until the restoration three decades later.[757] A gallery had been erected by 1850.[758]

The church was restored c.1876–7 to designs by J. Colson, under the direction of Francis J.E. Jervoise.[759] The church was greatly enlarged with the addition of a new north aisle, divided from the nave by an arcade of octagonal columns. A new tower was erected by Colson, who removed the entrance to the church from the south side of the nave to the south side of the tower. The 19th-century gallery was removed and new seats were installed, increasing the accommodation within the church to 250, although part of the Jervoise family pew dated 1634 was retained to serve as a screen for the organ.[760] At the same time one of his daughters presented the parish with a new font.[761] A reredos by Harry Hems was installed in 1884, whilst 20th-century stained glass windows by Hugh Powell in the nave commemorate members of the Jervoise family.[762] An extension of traditional appearance with washing and kitchen facilities was added in 2025.[763]

753 HRO, Will and inventory of William Hyde, 1549U/33.
754 HRO, 44M69/F2/14/28.
755 HRO, 44M69/F2/14/28.
756 HRO, Will of Edward Moore, 1641A/079.
757 HRO, 86M82/PV1, 13 Apr. 1841.
758 HRO, 86M82/PV1, 27 June 1850.
759 HRO, 44M69/J9/143; 86M82/PV1, Apr. 1877; *Kelly's Dir. Hants.* (1889 edn), 153.
760 NHLE, no. 1339500, 'Church of St Mary'.
761 *Kelly's Dir. Hants. (1885)*, 587.
762 *Pevsner North Hants.* 328; HRO, 21M65/192F.
763 Info. from Mr J. Jervoise, 2025.

LOCAL GOVERNMENT

Manorial Government

THERE ARE FEW extant records of manorial government on the manor of Herriard, although some records from the early 16th century do survive.[764] These often record the mundane everyday business of the manor, such as the registration of property conveyances, resolution of disputes over boundaries, and the presentment of nuisances and defective gates and hedges.[765] A parishioner was presented in 1623 for enclosing part of the common, and others for erecting cottages on the waste of the manor.[766] To prevent the overburdening of the commons, a counter of sheep was elected in the same year.[767] By the late 17th century only the business of the court baron, predominantly the conveyancing of property, was recorded.[768] Some tenants in the 1730s still owed capons to the lord besides sums of money for a relief before being admitted as tenant of a property.[769]

Southrope formed a separate tithing within the royal manor of Odiham, and the men of Southrope attended courts at Odiham in the late 14th century,[770] and still in 1844, where the year's constable and tithingman were selected, and cert money was paid.[771] Separate courts held at Southrope were recorded in the reign of Henry VIII,[772] and it was said in 1595 that separate courts were still kept twice a year within the hamlet. Officers of Odiham manor impounded strays in a pound within the tithing, and collected rents and fines belonging to the manor within Southrope. There was no pound in Herriard in the late 16th century, and the lord of Herriard had no power to deliver strays from the pound at Southrope.[773] Despite this, by the late 17th century Southrope was apparently accounted part of the manor of Herriard, with feudal dues

764 HRO, 44M69/A1/3/9–12; 44M69/E1/1/69; Magdalen College Oxford, Ct. Bk. 3.
765 HRO, 44M69/A1/3/1.
766 HRO, 44M69/A1/3/13.
767 HRO, 44M69/A1/3/13.
768 HRO, 44M69/A1/3/2.
769 HRO, 44M69/A1/3/2.
770 Harvard Law School Library, Odiham Hundred, Court Rolls, 1383, English Manor Rolls, Box 12, 89–93, 95: HOLLIS 11720694, https://id.lib.harvard.edu/ead/c/law00212c00198/catalog (accessed 4 Mar. 2025).
771 HRO, 25M63/M4–19.
772 HRO, 25M63/M5, ff. 9, 30, 40.
773 HRO, 44M69/F2/14/8.

such as heriots and reliefs paid by tenants in Southrope to the lord, whilst the homage made orders concerning the commons in Southrope.[774]

Parochial Government

A RATE LAID in the final years of the reign of Elizabeth I, for the relief of the impotent poor and the setting of other poor people to work, identified 27 adults and 40 children in need of support within the parish. It was signed by five leading parishioners, although it is unclear in what capacity these men signed the document.[775] A rate was laid in 1602 by two churchwardens and four overseers, levying a total of £4 10s. on the parish, from which £3 7s. 9d. was divided between five individuals.[776] Two overseers were named in a rate of Easter 1605, when £6 3s. 6d. was laid on the parish, to provide five parishioners weekly payment of between 6d. and 12d.[777] A sum of £3 15s. 7d. was levied at Easter 1607, when five poor widows received weekly payments of between 4d. and 6d. each, supplemented with extra payments to some of these women between Christmas and Easter.[778] Nevertheless, the local JP Edward Savage was compelled in June 1609 to order the Herriard overseers to make provision for three poor women who had complained to him that their families would starve because they received no relief from the parish.[779]

A select vestry had been established by the start of the 19th century,[780] and there is an extant minute book of its meetings from 1830. The routine work of the vestry comprised the appointment of parochial officers, the auditing of their accounts, the oversight of the school and parochial charities, and supervision of the roads. In February of that year the vestry ordered that 1,370 bundles, or bavins, of firewood should be distributed amongst the poor, because of the extreme severity of the weather. The wood was shared between 68 households in doles of between 15 and 25 bavins per household.[781] The vestry also determined that month that poor parishioners should be vaccinated against smallpox without delay.[782] Late in 1830 the vestry ordered an increase in weekly wages for labourers, from 9s. to 10s., with further payments of 2s. or more stipulated for households with at least three children, whilst the elderly were to receive 3s. a week. Orders were made for the employment of thirteen poor men by six employers in the parish, with the remainder, 'chiefly old men', ordered to be employed by the surveyor of the

774 HRO, 44M69/A1/3/2.
775 HRO, 44M69/J9/139.
776 HRO, 44M69/J9/136.
777 HRO, 44M69/J9/38.
778 HRO, 44M69/E4/6, f. 15v [second pagination].
779 HRO, 44M69/E4/6, f. 13 [second pagination].
780 HRO, 44M69/J9/59.
781 HRO, 86M82/PV1, 6 Feb. 1830.
782 HRO, 86M82/PV1, 12 Feb. 1830.

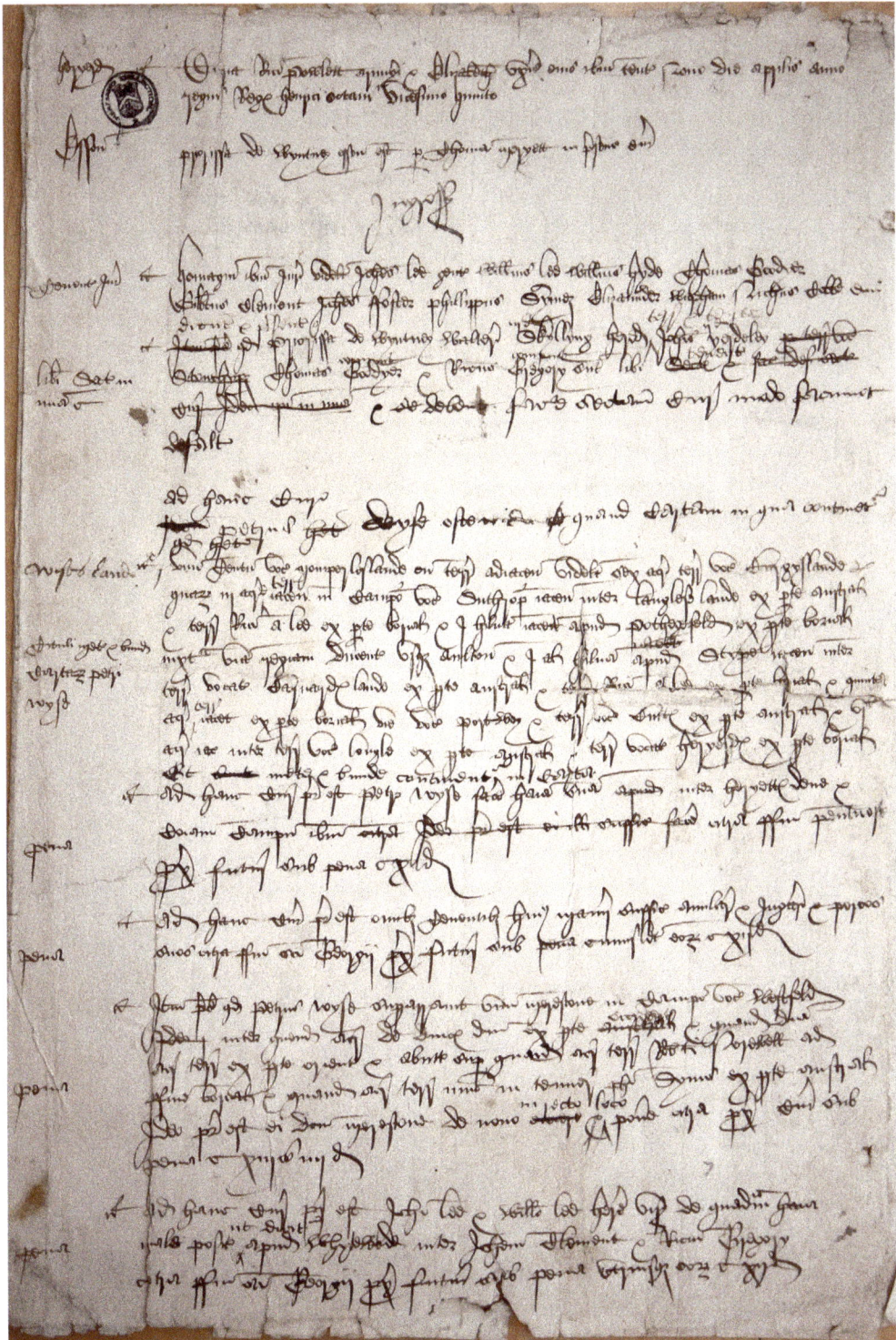

Fig. 43. Court rolls of Herriard manor, 1534. HRO, 44M69/A1/3/12.

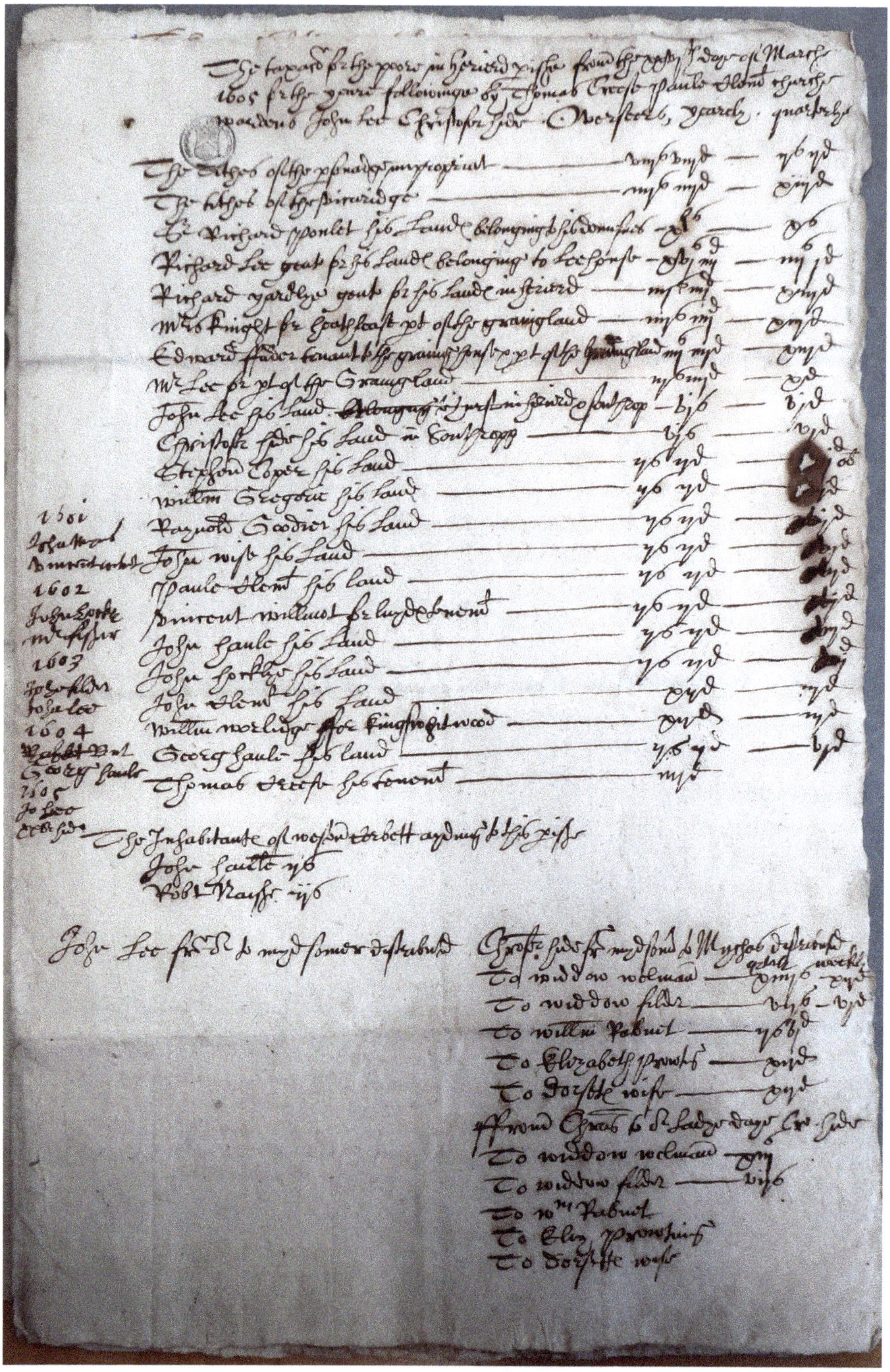

Fig. 44. A poor rate levied in 1605, with a list of payments to poor persons. HRO, 44M69/J9/38.

highways.[783] At a meeting in January 1833 the vestry supported a proposal that landowners within the parish should provide small quantities of land as allotments for the use of poor cottagers within the parish. More bavins were donated at that date by the lord of the manor for the support of the poor, and a concern was expressed about the best means to employ the extra labourers who were at that time numerous.[784]

A Herriard, Lasham and Tunworth Association for Prosecuting Felons was established in 1829, with punishments ranging from 10 gns for stealing livestock to 1 gn. for breaking a hedge.[785] In the following year, as rioting broke out in many parts of the county, George Purefoy Jervoise placed an order for 100 truncheons for special constables. In the event none of his tenants took part in the Captain Swing riots, for which Jervoise rewarded them at the end of the year with gifts of between 1s. and 10s. per household, amounting to more than £12 in Herriard.[786] A police officer was stationed at Herriard but was removed before 1858. Although it was reported that this made neighbouring beats too large and inefficient, no alterations were proposed at that date.[787] A police cottage was erected next to the school in the early 1950s.[788]

The parish was placed within the Basingstoke rural district sanitary authority, which became the Basingstoke rural district council in 1894.[789] Francis M.E. Jervoise, the lord of the manor, was elected the first district councillor for the parish, as well as one of the five members of the newly constituted parish council for Herriard.[790] Following the nomination of the initial councillors, without opposition, in 1894, selection of new councillors has always been by co-option, without elections ever having been held in the parish. Membership tended to be drawn from the leading farmers in the parish, with members of the Jervoise family usually taking the chair.[791] The parish council took on many of the responsibilities formerly held by the vestry, including the appointment of officers. In 1899 the council negotiated with the secretary of the General Post Office for the addition of money order and savings services at the village post office, and the installation of telegraph facilities.[792] The capital of a village nursing scheme, made redundant by the advent of the NHS, was dedicated in 1954 by the parish council to the erection of a bus shelter and the extension of the British Legion Hall.[793] Proposals were made

783 HRO, 86M82/PV1, 6 Dec. 1830. See also HRO, 44M69/J9/77.

784 HRO, 44M69/J9/25.

785 HRO, 86M82/PV1.

786 HRO, 44M69/E13/12/122.

787 *Hants. Ad.*, 15 Nov. 1862.

788 HRO, 63M83/B24/82.

789 F.A. Youngs, *Local Administrative Units of England* (London, 1979), I, 210.

790 *Hants & Berks. Gaz.* 8 Dec. 1894.

791 Owen White, unpubl. hist. of Herriard, *c.*2002.

792 Owen White, unpubl. hist. of Herriard, *c.*2002.

793 Owen White, unpubl. hist. of Herriard, *c.*2002.

in 1983 for the erection of eight bungalows for retired rural workers, completed in 1986 at Southrope Green.[794] Twenty years later, work was begun in the erection of six affordable homes. In the early 21st century the council has been keen to reduce the environmental impact of the parish, promoting renewable energy schemes, sustainable farming, and promoting green lifestyle changes.[795]

Complaints were made in 1881 about the poor maintenance of the roads between Herriard and Alton, which it was said was badly repaired with large rocks straight from the fields, and had not been metalled for some years.[796] Traction engines carrying ballast from Bradley to the railway station at Herriard caused serious damage to roads in the parish during construction of the railway,[797] and heavy motor lorries belonging to the L&SWR (operating in the place of the railway whose track had then been lifted) caused much damage in 1919.[798] Nevertheless, the roads were apparently still repaired with loose gravel and flint chippings until the 1920s, when they were first dressed with tarmac.[799] Roads were a frequent topic of concern for the parish council, who complained to the county council about areas liable to flooding and dangerous corners, some of which were not addressed until the 1980s.

Water supply in Herriard was problematic, as the parish stood 300 ft. above the level of local springs, leaving many residents dependent upon ponds and five deep wells sunk across the parish. In the late 19th century the issue was one of concern for the rural sanitary authority. The authority reported in 1878 that many residents resorted to ponds for water, none of which was fit for drinking.[800] Despite local objections, the medical officer of health returned to the issue in 1880, noting that residents in Back Lane had only stagnant pools for water supply, whilst a large tank installed at Park Corner was contaminated with animal and vegetable matter and so unfit for drinking.[801] More efficient and secure tanks to capture rainwater were installed in 1893 by the rural sanitary authority in a number of places across the parish.[802] Early in the 20th century a plentiful supply of water was discovered by a dowser at Lasham, and the Herriard Park estate soon established the Herriard & Lasham Water Company, supplying piped mains water to Herriard, Lasham, and nine neighbouring parishes.[803] Water was not supplied to individual homes, but

794 'Southrope Green', Anchor, https://www.anchor.org.uk/our-properties/southrope-green-basingstoke (accessed 4 Mar. 2025).
795 'Ecohub', Herriard Parish Council, https://herriard-pc.gov.uk/ecohub (accessed 4 Mar. 2025).
796 *Hants. Chron.* 5 Feb. 1881.
797 *Hants & Berks. Gaz.* 31 May 1902.
798 Owen White, unpubl. hist. of Herriard, *c*.2002.
799 Owen White, unpubl. hist. of Herriard, *c*.2002.
800 HRO, 44M69/E15/9.
801 HRO, 44M69/E15/10.
802 *Hants & Berks. Gaz.* 19 Aug. 1893; 29 Feb. 1896.
803 *The Times*, 28 May 1959; HRO, 44M69/E17/29; 44M69/E1/20/1–5.

to standpipes located in several places around the parish.[804] Under the terms of
the Mid-Wessex Water Order 1948, the Herriard & Lasham Water Company was
transferred to the Mid-Wessex Water Company on 1 Jan. 1949.[805]

804 Owen White, unpubl. hist. of Herriard, *c.*2002.
805 *Aldershot News*, 24 Mar. 1950.

ABBREVIATIONS

Abbreviations and short titles used include the following:

Abbreviation	Full text
a.	acre(s)
Abstract Pop. Rtns, 1801; 1833	*Abstracts of Population Returns* (Parl. Papers, 1801–2 (9), 1831 vi; 1833 (149), xxxvii)
Acts of PC	*Acts of the Privy Council of England* (HMSO, 1890–1964)
BDBC	Basingstoke and Deane Borough Council
BL	British Library
Book of Fees	*The Book of Fees* (HMSO, 1920–31)
Cal. Chart.	*Calendar of the Charter Rolls preserved in the Public Record Office* (HMSO, 1892–1963)
Cal. Close	*Calendar of the Close Rolls preserved in the Public Record Office* (HMSO, 1892–1963)
Cal. Cttee for Compounding	*Calendar of the Proceedings of the Committee for Compounding* (HMSO, 1889–92)
Cal. Inq. p.m.	*Calendar of Inquisitions post mortem preserved in the Public Record Office* (HMSO, 1904–2009)
Cal. Pat.	*Calendar of the Patent Rolls preserved in the Public Record Office* (HMSO, 1891–1986)
CCED	*The Clergy of the Church of England Database,* https://theclergy-database.org.uk/
Char. Com.	Charity Commission
Complete Peerage	G. E. C[okayne] and others, *The Complete Peerage* (2nd edn. 1910–59)
Compton Census	*The Compton Census of 1676: a Critical Edition,* ed. A. Whiteman (Records of Social and Economic History, n.s. 10, London, 1986)
Dioc. Pop. Rtns	*Diocesan Population Returns for 1563 and 1603,* ed. A. Dyer and D.M. Palliser (Records of Social and Economic History, n.s. 31, 2005)
Dir.	*Directory*
Doing the Duty	*Doing the Duty of the Parish: Surveys of the Church in Hampshire, 1810,* ed. M. Smith (HRS 17, 2004)
Domesday	*Domesday Book: a Complete Translation,* ed. A. Williams and G.H. Martin (London, 2002)
Dugdale, *Mon.*	W. Dugdale, *Monasticon Anglicanum,* ed. J. Caley and others (1817–30)

Educ. Enquiry Abstract	*Education Enquiry: Abstract of the Answers and Returns* (Parl. Papers, 1835 (62) i)
Educ. of Poor Digest	*Digest of Parochial Returns on the Education of the Poor (Parl. Papers, 1818 (224) ii)*
Ekwall, *English Place-Names*	E. Ekwall, *The Concise Oxford Dictionary of English Place-Names* (Oxford, 1951)
Excerpta e Rot. Finium	*Excerpta e Rotulis Finium, Hen. III*, 2 vols (Rec. Com., 1835–6)
f(f).	folio(s)
Feudal Aids	*Inquisitions and Assessments relating to Feudal Aids preserved in the Public Record Office*, 6 vols (HMSO, 1899–1920)
Gaz.	*Gazette*
Geol. Surv.	British Geological Survey
ha.	hectare(s)
Hants. Ad.	*Hants Advertiser*
Hants. Chron.	*Hampshire Chronicle*
HER	Hampshire Historic Environment Record, https://www.hants.gov.uk
Hants. Lay Subsidy, 1586	*The Hampshire Lay Subsidy Rolls, 1586* ed. C.R. Davey (HRS 4, 1981)
Hants. Tax List, 1327	*The Hampshire Tax List of 1327, ed. P. Mitchell-Fox and M. Page (HRS 20, 2014)*
HRO	Hampshire Record Office
HRS	Hampshire Record Series
Hearth Tax, 1665	*The Hampshire Hearth Tax Assessment, 1665*, ed. E. Hughes and P. White (HRS 11, 1991)
Hist. Parl.	*The History of Parliament (1964-)*
Kelly's Dir. Hants.	*Kelly's Directory of Hampshire and the Isle of Wight*
L&P Hen. VIII	*Letters and Papers, Foreign and Domestic, of the Reign of Henry VIII* (HMSO, 1864–1932)
Lon. Gaz.	*London Gazette*
LPL	Lambeth Palace Library, London
L&SWR	London & South Western Railway
Mapledurwell	J. Hare, J, Morrin and S, Waight, *Mapledurwell* (The Victoria History of Hampshire, 2012)
Medieval Basingstoke	J. Hare, *Basingstoke: a medieval town, c.1000–c.1600* (The Victoria History of Hampshire, 2017)
Nonarum Inquisitiones	*Nonarum Inquisitiones in Curia Scaccarii* (Rec. Com., 1807)
NHLE	National Heritage List for England, https://historicengland.org.uk/listing/the-list/
n.s.	new series

ODNB	*Oxford Dictionary of National Biography* (Oxford, 2004); https://www.oxforddnb.com
OS	Ordnance Survey
PRS	Pipe Roll Society
Parl. Papers	Parliamentary Papers
Parson and Parish	*Parson and Parish in Eighteenth Century Hampshire: Replies to Bishops' Visitations* (HRS 13, 1995)
Pevsner *North Hants.*	*The Buildings of England. Hampshire: Winchester and the North*, ed. M. Bullen, J. Crook, R. Hubbuck and N. Pevsner (London, 2010)
Pipe R.	Pipe Roll
Poor Law Abstract, 1804; 1818	*Abstract of Answers and Returns relative to the Expense and Maintenance of the Poor* (Parl. Papers, 1804 (175), i; 1818, (82), xix)
Poor Rate Rtns, 1830–1; 1835	*Select Committee on Poor Rate Returns: Reports* (Parl. Papers, 1830–1 (83), xi; 1835 (444), xlvii)
Proc. Hants F.C.	*Proceedings of the Hampshire Field Club and Archaeological Society*
Rec. Com.	Record Commission
Reg. Chichele	*The Register of Henry Chichele, Archbishop of Canterbury, 1414–1443*, ed. Jacob, 4 vols (Canterbury and York Society, 42, 45–7, 1938–47)
Reg. Langton	HRO, 21M65/A1/16: register of Thomas Langton
Reg. Pontissara	*Registrum Johannis de Pontissara, episcopi Wyntoniensis, 1282–1304*, ed. C. Deedes, 2 vols (Canterbury and York Society, 19 and 30, 1915–24)
Regs. Sandale and Asserio	*John de Sandale and Rigaud de Asserio AD 1316–1325. Episcopal Registers: Diocese of Winchester*, ed. F.J. Baigent (HRS, 1897)
Reg. Woodlock	*Registrum Henrici Woodlock, Diocesis Wintoniensis, A.D. 1305–1316*, ed. A.W. Goodman. 2 vols (Canterbury and York Society, 43–4, 1940–1).
Reg. Wykeham	*Wykeham's Register*, ed. T.F. Kirby, 2 vols (HRS, 1896–9)
Rel. Census, 1851	*The Religious Census of 1851*, ed. J.A. Vickers (HRS 12, 1993)
Rep. Com. Council on Educ. 1882–3; 1883–4; 1884–5; 1891–2; 1897–8	*Reports of the Committee of Council on Education (England and Wales)* (Parl. Papers, 1883[C.3706], xxv; 1884 [C.4091], xxiv; 1884–5 [C.4483], lx; 1892[C.6746], xxviii; 1898 [C.8989], lxix)
rot.	rotulus
Tax. Eccl.	*Taxatio Ecclesiastica Angliae et Walliae auctoritate Papae Nicholai IV, c.1291* (Rec. Com. 1802)
TNA	The National Archives

www.ingramcontent.com/pod-product-compliance
Lightning Source LLC
Chambersburg PA
CBHW061408090426
42740CB00024B/3476